Morning Messages

from Mary

Illuminating the Path to a Life without Edges

Morning Messages

from Mary

Illuminating the Path to a Life without Edges

Jacque Nelson

RADIANT HEART PRESS
Milwaukee, Wisconsin

Published with delight by
Radiant Heart Press
An imprint of HenschelHAUS Publishing, Inc.
2625 S. Greeley Street, Suite 201
Milwaukee, WI 53207
www.HenschelHAUSbooks.com

Please contact the publisher for quantity discounts.

ISBN: 978-1-59598-126-4
LCCN: 2011922521
Library of Congress Cataloging in Publication data available on request.

Cover photograph by Don Nelson, "Barefoot Coffee, Nosara, Costa Rica"

Cover design by Kevin Gardner

Printed in the United States of America.

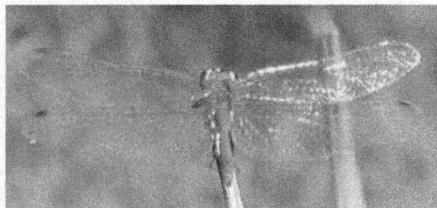

Loving whispers landing on the air
like dragonfly wings you will find me there

This book is dedicated in loving memory
to our dear, beautiful friend, Ginny Erlandsson,
a great teacher of courage, laughter, and love.

Acknowledgements

So many amazing beautiful people have offered love, enthusiasm and encouragement to me in this journey with Mary that it would be impossible to name them individually. Telling each one of them who they are to me and expressing my appreciation for what they have gifted to me that has made it possible to expand this beautiful work, finally produce this book and the ones to follow, could be a whole book in itself. So, I will just say, "Thank you to every soul who has ever graced me with touching mine with love and belief."

I do wish to offer a very special note of my deepest gratitude to my love, my friend, my true companion, Donald Nelson, my husband. Without your embrace, gentle and insistent nudging, your vision, your passion and

your belief in me and the work we do with Mary, I may have let this incredible gift slip away unutilized for all that it is. Thank you for always cheering me on and knowing with all certainty what we have to offer to the world. I love you.

I would also be remiss in not expressing specific heart-drenching appreciation to my two beautiful children Michelle and Dustin, who were willing to grow up in an "unusual" household and share me with Mary and all who come to talk with them. I recognize that they have sacrificed having had more of my time and attention and "normalcy" in our way of life. I can only hope that the immense love that this life has produced in me and in our world of kindred spirits has offered them more than they would have ever known without it. They are both beautiful and inspiring and I love them more than I can express.

–Jacque Nelson

How it all began ...

These wisdoms and Mary have been weaving their way into every aspect of our lives since March of 2000.

Prior to that time, my husband Don and I had been living pretty mainstream lives; Don had worked in the printing industry for twenty years and I was a human resource director for a mid-sized not-for-profit organization. While we both knew we wanted to step "out of the box" with our lives and our work, we had no idea, until the day that Mary began moving and speaking through me, that this would be our path.

An intuitive counselor and metaphysical teacher with whom Donald had a conversation back then suggested that Don and I sit together and meditate for five minutes a day. We were to focus on bringing through the guidance we were seeking, to help us know what we might do with our lives, and so we began. Don had been meditating on and

off since he was eleven. At that point in my life, I had no self-discipline for such things, so five minutes seemed doable and non-threatening. I had no idea that those five minutes would completely change my life in every possible way.

As Don and I sat for the meditation the first time, I closed my eyes, asked my mind to quiet and began to feel the stillness of my body, sensing its weight against the surface I was lying on. Then, my face started to move about—on its own—wincing, contorting, and stretching. While that seemed a bit odd, I just figured it was part of meditation. After mentioning the experience to Don after we were complete, I learned that, at least for him, such an experience was not typical.

The second time we sat to meditate, the same movement of my face began immediately, followed by a bit of flailing of my limbs and strong messages about kinesiology running through my head. While admittedly it was a bit odd to experience, with Don thinking that perhaps I just could not be still for even five minutes for meditation, it all actually seemed quite natural and a bit fascinating to both of us.

The third day when we lay down to meditate again, the movement in my physical body accelerated immediately and I received a strong message to sit up. At that point, I knew the message was not coming *from* me, but instead it was coming *through* me. Being a bit stubborn and needing some confirmation that what was happening was really happening, I responded not by sitting my body up but by saying, "If you want to sit me up, you will have to do it yourself."

Don had been distracted from his meditation by all the commotion and sat up to stare at me. He describes what he saw to be like there was an invisible string attached to my chest pulling my body up from the mattress while my arms hung limp on either side of my torso. There were three or four attempts, with my body dropping back down to the mattress before I was finally in an upright, seated position.

Now, you might want to remember that while we were looking for something a bit different, this was WAY different and yet all truly seemed so natural. It was as if when "they" came through, "they" gave us an instantaneous and innate understanding and peace about the

exchange. All I have ever felt when the group of spiritual entities we now refer to as Mary, or the Mary Group, or simply "they" comes through—is pure, beautiful, radiant love.

Once they sat me up, they were off and running, moving about the room on my feet, my knees, and even rolling my body around the floor. Once the movement of my body was figured out, they began to speak with us, offering expansive wisdom, grand insight, and constantly birthing joy for the human experience.

They haven't stopped since. They come whenever we ask and sometimes nudge us to let them share something inspiring, affirming, or enlightening when we don't. It has been the most magical and transforming journey I can imagine having.

Living Mary's Wisdoms and bringing them to the world has intrinsically ignited life for Don and me. Internally and externally. Each time I shift a thought or belief and feel my life open or I receive a story from another who has felt a complete transformation of something that had painfully stagnated his or her life before, I feel that if such alterations were the only outcome from all

of this, it would be enough. Yet, there are hundreds of these moments, these stories, these transformations that have come to us resulting from conversations and guidance provided by Mary. We are so grateful and so excited to share them with you.

—Jacque and Don Nelson

Dear Friend,

Because this book truly holds an impeccable power to open you to the incredibly magical world inside of you, where all of your dreams already know you and all of your most extraordinary, life-giving choices and awakenings thrive, we encourage you to create a conscious practice around your use of its significance. It is a compelling tool to transformation.

You can choose to simply flip through the pages, land on one of the messages, read it and then move about your day. This way of being with the book and yourself will offer you a very nice moment and perhaps a catalyst to embark on your day with a deepened sense of well-being, an expanded contemplative thought, or a tantalizing new perspective. Or, you can choose, instead, to go a bit deeper,

allowing the sleeping giant inside of you to be seen, touched and revealed to you through the awakening vibration that these messages contain. If you choose this path, we encourage you to create a practice of setting aside a few minutes of time each day to consciously hold this book in your hands, take in a deep, long, slow, clearing breath (alerting your whole being that you are choosing pure life), allow yourself to be completely present unlocking within you, a drenching state of peace.

Then, call forth your intuition to guide you to the page that holds the perfect combination of words and vibration for you on that day, that when taken in deeply, has the power to elicit edgeless openings and understandings within you. In that moment, while the words and vibration are swirling around inside of you, make a commitment to yourself and your life, to live the message out loud with all your might, all your joy, and all your celebration. You may even choose to make enough time in your practice to journal or jot down thoughts that move through you in association with the message and what it moves and stimulates in you.

If on the next day, you are ready to move onto a new message, then repeat this process. If you do not yet feel complete with the message from the day before and wish to continue to live in the vibration and exploration of it so that you may receive a more thorough understanding and experience of it, then stay with that one each day until you feel it really sync with you, offering its full potential for your desired manifestation of real transformation.

This book, this tool utilized in this way, in partnership with your will to let yourself have its gifts, offers you the opportunity for the full experience of an edgeless, ecstatic life. Many blessings.

With pure love,
Mary

L et's make a deal or two today. You open your heart and we will climb inside and stoke the fire. You open your mind and we will offer opportunities to expand it. You open your soul and we will weave ourselves into union with you. You open your spirit and we will put on our gear and take the co-pilot seat.

Together again. Let's fly,
Mary

We see you there, standing on the precipice of a Brand New Beginning. We invite you to allow your vision to span the horizon of all possibility and we encourage you to move forward into it, taking with you that which embraces, celebrates, and inspires you and leaving behind that which separates, denies, and depletes you.

Still finding you breathtaking,
Mary

P.S. Oh, by the way, we have checked our list of most desirable people to hang out with this year and you are definitely on it. We sure hope we make your "most desirable spirits to hang out with" list. Because, kid, this could be the continuation of a beautiful relationship ...

E very day, every day, without fail, trust.

Something, anything ... just trust.

And the next day, trust more. And so on. Start where it feels truthful for you and build from there.

Void of doubt,
Mary

egin and continue. With anything you wish to accomplish, everything you wish to experience. Begin and continue.

Simple really,
Mary

Anytime your thoughts are not bringing you happiness today, think something else. Invent new or different thoughts about the same thing you are already mulling around or think about something else all together that brings that pleasure-filled smile to your face that we are so fond of.

Go ahead, just try it. Everybody is doing it ...

You really are in charge, you know ... of yourself, that is,
Mary

We encourage you to give yourself opportunity to enjoy the freedom and release that forgiveness brings to you when you offer it to yourself and others.

Real (**R**adiating **E**dgelessness-**A**llowing **L**ove) forgiveness.

Live free,
Mary

We nudge you to notice and feel the immensity of all that is good in your life today. Then, allow yourself to swirl it through you in an elegant or even excited dance with all that feels good within you. Let the result be the vibration you source yourself through as you choose how you show up for your moments in your life today. Oh, and tomorrow, and the next day and so on, if you choose, too.

Admiring the light in your eyes,
Mary

Sometimes, the life you are creating, choice by choice, moment by moment, calls on you to use your courage and vision to change your course and step into your true greatness.

Behind you all the way,
Mary

You know those little scrapes and bruises you get on your body from time to time? They are very similar in nature to the ones you get on the inside of you. It's just that sometimes, you allow the wounds on the inside to fester and get infected so they don't heal as fast as the ones on the outside. Or you keep picking the scab until it leaves a scar that stays with you.

We invite you to consider letting the little scrapes and bruises to your feelings heal by applying tender loving care and maybe some soothing salve to yourself to promote a speedy recovery. Just saying ...

Big, big love,
Mary

ove and set free the lover in you today. Go ahead, open yourself up to sharing that immense heart of yours with the world. Give with no anticipation of getting anything back and yet with complete knowing that you will. Perhaps not from where you offered it and instead from somewhere else, maybe even yourself.

Oh, love looks so good in you,
Mary

Today, we invite you to let one thousand thoughts, one thousand minutes, one thousand words and one thousand heart beats swirl with and emanate your belief in your dreams. Yes, it is very important that you believe in your dreams.

Whether they are large or small, long-term or short-term, dreams all need to be fed by their dreamer to manifest and thrive.

One thousand eyes of love gazing at you,
Mary

Sometimes, miracles come in what might be considered by the human mind operating alone, deceptive ways. However, when you add your heart, soul, and spirit to the viewing and absorbing equation, allowing these miracles to sink in and give you what they came to offer, it all becomes very clear.

And, the thing is, these miracles are happening all of the time.

Open, realize, and receive yours,
Mary

Today is a good day to ...

... Believe with all your might

... Love with all your heart

... Fly with all your fuel

... Dream with all your imagination

... Know with all your wisdom

... Shine with all your light

Of, course, so was yesterday and so will tomorrow be ...

Let 'er rip,
Mary

We encourage you to practice kindness today. At every turn, through every word, in all of your exchanges, internally and externally.

Kindness is one of your aspects that carries a significant vibration-shifting energy that opens you and assists us with smoothing out the "rough spots," large and small.

In this together,
Mary

We encourage you to let hope pierce all of your moments today.

Honing Optimum Possibility Energy about EVERYTHING.

Everything,
Mary

Today, know that you are stronger and more clever than whatever it is you are wrestling with inside ... current depleting thoughts, derailing practices, choices that don't line up with your desired state of existence ... yep, stronger and more clever than all of them! This truth really does stand to reason, since you are the one who created these thoughts, practices, and choices in the first place.

So, when you get tired of wrestling, let them know you have decided to win and get on with embodying who you choose to be now. Just a suggestion.

Loving you grandly,
Mary

Dreaming, Streaming, Beaming ... Yes, Yes, Yes! Consider making today a day of grand practice of all of them!

Yowsa!
Mary

Consider putting your face fully into the world today. Oh, and if you choose to do so, make sure that what is lighting your eyes, igniting your smile, and generating the breath that makes your nostrils flare ever so slightly, as you inhale and exhale through that exquisite nose of yours, is YOU.

Show up in your life today, as yourself deeply and clearly influenced by what in each moment feels the yummiest in you.

Twirling in our love for you,
Mary

Stand up and stretch your arms upward and outward as far as you can reach. Let yourself feel your body lengthen and open wide for a brand-new day. Then, close your eyes, inhale and exhale deeply, and do the same thing on the inside, allowing the full stretch of your invitation to life to reach up and out to all it can possibly touch and take in today.

It just feels good.

Whistling and humming,
Mary

L isten today. Not with your opinion and judgment (preconceived or newly forming) at the ready, and instead, with your curiosity and exploration fully engaged.

It's titillating.

Always more,
Mary

Offer yourself an extraordinary day today. Then, open wide and let yourself in.

After all, you wouldn't want to miss out on such a thing would you?

Skipping and singing,
Mary

Won't you join us?

Today, we encourage you to allow yourself to recognize the beauty in all things, to feel and know the wisdom that lives and moves within you and to experience the love that flows abundantly in all of your moments.

Floating in the abyss of your essence,
Mary

Travel within and take yourself to the pulsing light of whatever vibration opens and inspires you today. Go ahead, pick out your favorite outfit and accessories (the aspects that fit you most deliciously), spiff yourself up a bit (clean up any inward and outward dishonoring, careless or limiting thoughts, words, actions that you have been practicing), select your transportation (ride on the wave of love, joy, belief, wonder, amazement ...) and arrive there with commitment.

Then, take the time to really take it all in. Mesmerize yourself in the wonder of this pulsing light, let it move in and through you soaking you thoroughly in it's vibrational match to you becoming one in union with you and soar, soar.

Always loving you,
Mary

What are you participating in? Pay attention to what you are choosing to involve yourself in today—internal thoughts, external conversations, and activities. Notice which of these things activate and celebrate your desired state of existence and which ones deflate it. Then ... decide.

Go forth and create,
Mary

W hat will you let into your experience of you today?

Joy ... Clarity ... Love ... Passion ... Delight ... Worry ... Caution ... Bursting ... Ecstasy ... Harmony ... Belief ... Struggle ... Strength ... Awkwardness ... Magic ... Union ... Lack ... Peace ... Truth ... Purpose ... Magnificence ... Humor ... Integrity ... Playfulness ...

Whichever and however many you choose, invite the gift they offer to you, swim in your gratitude for them, and keep moving onto the next and the next and the next. And remember ... you can let more than one in at a time.

Invigorating Possibility,
Mary

What ulterior motives are you currently practicing? You know ... the motivators that lurk in the background of the things that you do, think, and act out. Check to see what these are, be completely honest with yourself about them and decide if they are a match to your vision of you and how you wish to share yourself in your world. Do they come from an open, illuminating space or a tight, threatened space? How do you feel as you are catalyzed by them?

Just tell yourself the truth, Decide to keep them or shift them and move forth with your creating.

Freeing the spaces that bind you,
Mary

Tra-la-la. When was the last time you practiced yourself in a light, easy, wistfully delightful vibration? One filled with promise, anticipation, exuberance, and whimsy.

Good. Then do it again. Longer this time.

With a lilt in our step,
Mary

Move like a stream in its moment-to-moment flow today, instinctively knowing your direction. Even if you are unclear about the destination, you know what way to flow while moving over, around, and in harmony with all things in your path.

Ahhhhhh,
Mary

nhale deeply, breathing in life, creation, and infinite possibilities. Point your nose in any direction and choose something there to breathe deeply into your experience. Let it swirl and linger within you and then release your breath, offering your celebration of it back out into the world. And repeat.

All together now,
Mary

You are an astounding human. Yes, you. Rich in love and cleverness. Echoing in passion and curiosity. Zooming in delight and wonder. Roaring in purpose and excellence. Emanating light and possibility. Galloping with zest and depth. Swimming in thoughts and creations. Radically traversing old boundaries and edges. Excelling in pleasure and exploration. Perfecting open heart and open mind. Commanding choice and deliberateness. Enhancing life and celebration. Charging forward in hope and truth. Sizzling in wisdom and whiles. Leaping in joy and abandon. Lingering in contemplation and caring. Saturating in becoming and satisfaction. Awakening with allowing and release. Birthing imagination and peace. Wrestling ... Triumphing ... Choosing ... Becoming ... Dancing ... Easing ... Screaming ... Dreaming ...

And the beat goes on,
Mary

We invite you to choose a feeling that feels good—really, really good—pulsing, swirling, expanding, delicious even, and stick with it today. Meet every thought, every word offered and received, every moment, every exchange, every action, every response ... with it. It may take some concerted effort, some commitment, some deliberate choosing and some releasing, rearranging, and reinvention of yourself to do this.

We say, "Go for it. You are worth it."

Your life, with you in charge,
Mary

Right now, wonderfully ecstatic stars are coming together with great precision and thrill to blend their vibration with yours in celebration of the fire, the sparkle, the glow that you brought with you to fill the world with. Are you willing to join them at the party and unleash your light, your brilliance, your shine, full on into your world, your life, and everything in it?

Oh, we do hope so!

We have our party shoes and dance floor wings on,
Mary

C hange is hard. Or ... it is not hard at all. Maybe it is even inspiring, life-expanding, or thrilling. You decide.

We love the way you move,
Mary

ow is the time for you to love yourself with all your might, believe in yourself with all your strength, and celebrate yourself with all your vigor. Why would you wait? Remember, what you give to yourself, you have available in equal measure to share with others. Be a giant.

Now, more than before,
Mary

We encourage you to go hog wild today. Full steam ahead. Launch into your day through your aspects of complete belief, streaming joy and outrageous possibility. Put your "life battery" on full charge. Let 'er rip. Birth, explore, discover, offer a rampage on all you love in life to yourself and somebody else, thrill, chortle, embrace ...

Live!
Mary

W hat is your current relationship with your aspect of confidence? How do you move with it? When and where do you call on it? Do you open to its response? What kind of friendship do you share with it? Constant companion, good-times buddy, deep and abiding, somewhat illusive?

We encourage you to invite your confidence to hang out with you today in every thought, in every word, in every dream, in every passion, in every action, in every exchange, in every moment. If you choose to do so, go ahead now, close your eyes, breathe deeply into yourself, with each breath invite your confidence to rise inside of you and expand into all of your particles. Let yourself open to its stirring and presence and take it out into the world with you to whatever degree you choose to summon it. Look through its eyes, feel through its vibration, respond through its wisdom ... if it feels good. It is always up to you.

Loving you without reservation,
Mary

What will you plant in your internal garden today? What seeds will you turn into your soil to make ready for fertile growth?

What weeds will you pull to assure your new growth has plenty of unencumbered ground to flourish in and gets all of the nutrients you have to offer?

Love to watch you grow,
Mary

Stretch today. Go ahead, release a big yawn, and elongate your body from the tips of your toes to the tips of your fingers outstretched over your head and flailing around a bit. With this fine movement, feel your physical body enjoy the fine rush of all of your cells being reminded that you are alive and have even a deeper breath to pull from and a more stimulating reach to experience. Follow that by rubbing the palms of your hands together in great anticipation of what you will create in the day ahead of you. Add your inner grin to this exercise and you are off to an incredible, delicious, alive, filled-by-you day!

Enjoy!
Mary

What causes your belief in something or someone? Is it your thought process and analyzing or your wisdom and knowing? We invite you to pay attention to where you believe from today. You may notice that you believe from each or from both combined, depending on the nature of the thing or your relationship with the person you are considering. Just notice what causes your belief from inside of you and outside of you. Your beliefs are some of the main drivers of your rhythm, your creating. It is good to know where they take their direction from.

If you choose to contemplate this today, remember to ask yourself questions and not question yourself about it. It will be much more enlightening and expanding that way.

Getting to know you, Getting to know all about you ... (la,la,la)
Mary

We encourage you to take out the garbage today. All of the junk thoughts that fill your mind. All of the rubbish that clogs your flow. All of the waste that drains your energy. Put it on the curb, blow it a kiss as you walk away, and breathe in your new possibility.

Loving you,
Mary

Today, may you give yourself opening to more love, more belief, more joy, more understanding, more pleasure, more inspiration, more peace, more courage, more passion, more life, more friendship, more beauty, more allowing, more recognition, more harmony, more grinning, more inner light bursting, more breath ... than you ever have before.

Always more,
Mary

Y our life is full of amazing moments. For instance, the moment you are in right now. Today, we invite you to notice your moments through the aspect of Inspired.

Examples: This moment inspires me to embrace the beauty within and around me ... This moment inspires me to change something in me and in my life ... This moment inspires me to reach into a greater sense of myself and reach out to share it ... This moment inspires me to be very creative in my response to it ... This moment inspires me to embrace change and learn of its gifts ... This moment inspires me to love more and judge less so that I may feel better ... This moment inspires me to release my current relationship with fear ... This moment inspires me to embrace the full volume of my gratitude and puff it up even bigger ...

Offering you edgeless and endless opportunities,
Mary

Morning Messages from Mary

Have you ever noticed that when you consistently overstretch elastic it may hold out for a while and then it begins to come apart, snapping in places and losing its ability to "bounce back" when released from the stretch. Or when you have used it well, off and on, say in a waistband, for a long time and then put it away in a drawer for so long that the next time you pull it out you find that it has dried up and no longer has flexibility?

Hmmm. Where might you be overextending yourself and breaking apart? And where might you be leaving your ability to be beneficially flexible and expandable put away for so long that you are becoming stagnant?

Isn't it interesting how your outside world reflects your inside world in the most seemingly innocent and often unnoticed ways?

Inviting you to practice your perfect stretch, flexibility and expandability,
Mary

Today and every day, we invite you to consciously treat yourself the way you treat others.

If you are warm, caring, and allowing with them, be warm, caring and allowing with yourself.

If you are short-tempered, unkind, and controlling with them, be short-tempered, unkind, and controlling with yourself.

If you are ignited and inspired in your belief in them and their dreams, be ignited and inspired in your belief in yourself and your dreams.

If you love them with great celebration, adoring, and embrace, love yourself with great celebration, adoring, and embrace.

Then, as a result of the experience, make some choices about how you will treat others and yourself as you move forward.

You are always choosing ...
Mary

Go on a bender of love today.

Completely intoxicate yourself with every flavor and form of it you can get your heart on and in, coming from the inside and the outside. Bedazzle yourself in the way it makes your head feel light and tingly, your spirit feel like dancing and your inhibitions lose their edges.

Now that is a high with no hangover!

Celebrating with you,
Mary

L IVE your moments today. All of them. Take you abundantly with you into your day. Make yourself your own guest of honor or MVP in your life. And, through your words, actions, and vibrational invitation, encourage others to be the guest of honor or MVP in their own lives also.

Puff up a bit, spread the wealth of you, and receive the wealth of others into your life.

It's a great party,
Mary

Wthout a sound, let somebody know that he or she is appreciated and important to you. Do something "special" for the other. No matter how large or small your action is, it will gift you and the other person immensely.

We suggest you begin with you and then move on to the next, then the next, then the next.

Edgeless love,
Mary

Today, we invite you to consider speaking only positive words about yourself and others. Only say things about yourself that you would truly like to hear others say about you.

You may have to cut out things like, "I am so stupid" and "My thighs are so fat." Unless you would like to have somebody else tell you that you are stupid or that you have fat thighs, that is. And, only say things about others that you would like to have them hear you say about them if they were right there with you. Do whatever it takes to keep all of the other words from coming out of your mouth. We suggest you use your love to help dissipate them.

Then tomorrow, step it up a notch and consider thinking only positive thoughts about yourself and others.

Since your thoughts feed your words and your words feed your thoughts, this will be very helpful to you in being joyfully successful in the practice of only speaking positive words.

The result, of course, is more inner peace and enormous relief from a practice that may be draining you instead of filling you.

Negativity never feeds you, though you may sometimes convince yourself that it does. That is why it is called negativity, because it takes away from you and your world. Otherwise it would be called "additivity."

Just a little spring cleaning,
Mary

ake a moment now to think of somebody or something that inspires you to smile. You know, the kind of deep, appreciating smile that makes the corners of your eyes crinkle. Then carry that smile around inside of you all day, living your moments through it, by sharing it with yourself and others.

Seems like a rather delicious way to enjoy a day from our perspective.

For love,
Mary

Introduce yourself to something new or unusual for you today. Choose a new experience, a new thought, response, gesture, endeavor ...

Take a different way to work or play, offer a warm hello to somebody you usually just pass by, get out of the other side of your bed, look up a word you never use and use it, touch trees and the earth every chance you get, let out a roar of joy or release, twirl instead of walk, free your laughter to know you where it hasn't lately, be as kind and patient with yourself as you are with others ...

Dance!
Mary

We invite you to dip into your sense of possibility today. To whatever measure you choose, dip in and move with it. Get it on everything. See through its eyes. Experience through its vibration. Breath through its flow. Create through its infinity.

Relish!
Mary

S timulate and elevate your senses today. Consider allowing yourself to enjoy life through them with great invitation. Smell. Touch. See. Hear. Taste. Vibrate with a heightened awareness. Right now, and several times throughout your day, invite yourself to really notice your moments through all of these arenas. Or, choose one or two at a time and experience the added significance and richness that each offers you in your infinitely possible exchange with the world.

Soaking you in,
Mary

Disentangle yourself from limited thought, stifling belief, and dodgy excuses today. How? you ask. Choose to.

When something inside of you feels confining or restrictive, infuse it with your choice to open, love, explore, expand, be free, discover ... you get the picture. Let it know that great change is coming and then create that change through always moving toward and through that which you do want, instead of stewing in that which you find no longer a match to you. On the inside first and then the outside.

Lovingly offering the keys to release the shackles,
Mary

B efore you do anything else, take a moment now to put the palm of your hand on your heart, draw in a deep, centering breath and say, "I am in love with me"... and repeat that several times.

If it resonates as true, wonderful! If it does not resonate as true, wonderful! Both are very revealing to you. Either way, we invite you to spend the rest of your day noticing and embracing moments of you to enjoy, adore, celebrate, and value. Moments as simple as noticing that you are a highly skilled tooth-brusher to moments as infinitely impacting as having a string of kind or loving thoughts, words, and actions that you share with yourself and others.

Take yourself with you today. Treat yourself to the kind of friendship you offer to others.

Admiring your beauty and bountiful possibility,
Mary

Where will you take yourself today? Internally and externally. What will you open to? How much love are you willing to receive and offer as you move through this day? In how many spaces and moments are you ready to recognize its availability and desire to know you well?

We invite you to take yourself by the hand, by the heart, and by the soul today and embark on your life. Open to your magic, wonder, amazement, and passion and live vibrantly, vividly, and deliberately.

You're so cute when you are zoomy like that!
Mary

Express yourself today. Let other people know how much they mean to you. Share with others your insight of the intricate importance and joyful impact you recognize their presence in your world and your life as having.

Go ahead and let them know expecting nothing back from them. Just saturate in the feeling of having shared something so beautiful from within you with somebody outside of you.

Talk about a quick high,
Mary

What could you benefit from trusting more today? Yourself, your skill, your vision, your belief, your innate wisdom, your _____? We invite you to fill in the blank and offer at least one more particle (perhaps thousands more particles) of trust to it today and feel the shift it creates within you.

Believing in you all the way!
Mary

P.S. Do you need a little kick start? Just think of how it feels to have somebody else place his or her trust in you (not expectation, trust—big difference). Remember how it makes you feel and how it sparks your enthusiasm to meet that trust. Give that to yourself. More than once if you feel so inclined.

Try these on for size:

"I am beautiful." "I am a victim." "I am infinite." "I am not enough." "I am a giant." "I am struggling." "I am love." "I am incapable." "I am delicious."

Which ones most often fit the story you are writing about yourself with every breath that you create in? Pay attention and realptime edit well, to arrive at "The End" having lived the life you desire. Remember, living your life from the inside out, choosing how you show up for your moments, no matter what they are, is what assures you great success.

Autograph please!
Mary

Take good care of yourself today. Go ahead, tend to your every need, nurture yourself inside and out. Lovingly embrace and celebrate you. Go out of your way to be nice to you, to be encouraging to you. Give yourself your time and attention and spoil you oh so "rotten." Applaud and praise your accomplishments and listen openly and admiringly to your visions and dreams. Believe in you without reason or proof of deserving, and instead, do it just because you choose to. Wrap yourself in your most beautiful love and tenderness and sink into you with pure joy.

Or not.

You decide.

Purely,
Mary

Morning Messages from Mary

In the moments that you feel like you want to run away from your life, how about you run directly into it with you fully engaged instead? We find it very interesting that many times, when "things" feel a bit overwhelming internally or externally, humans tend to want to escape, avoid, withdraw, or hide. What would happen if every time a challenge large or small manifested, you pulled up your confidence, your curiosity, your trust, your imagination, your peace, your initiative, your insight ... and moved full steam ahead into the challenge with you intact?

Oh, we know the answer. You would be there with you ... by your side ... supporting and encouraging yourself ... believing in you ... taking the driver's seat and steering wheel for your life into your own hands ... making choices about how you move through your moments and who you are becoming and how you will show up and how you will share yourself with life ... your life. Hmmmmm ...

Woo-hoo! Who would want to miss out on that?!
Mary

Y ou are living in amazing times. The current of change is in the air and moving swiftly. We invite you to open to the understanding that sometimes the angst or the emotional and even physical pain you or others may be experiencing is due to something you or they are trying to keep the same when change is inevitable.

When the collective is manifesting change to move swiftly, such as it is now, and you are attempting to remain the same in something you cling to or in the circumstances or experiences that surround you, the intensity of the angst or the pain increases to get you to let go and be free of whatever it is that is holding you back.

Oh, and remember, what holds you back is always about how you are thinking, choosing, and showing up on the inside, not what it is connected to on the outside.

Before you can fly with great precision and exquisite
freedom in the gently or strongly moving currents, you
have to let go of or shift whatever old or new fear or
pattern it is that you are using to keep you tethered inside.
Once you have done this, you will naturally find what does
and does not match you on the outside.

One particle at a time or thousands. You choose.
Mary

Do something out of the ordinary today. Give yourself permission to howl or twirl. Or perhaps for you, out of the ordinary would be to still yourself for a moment, breathe in and out deeply, and fully and invite calm and peace into your awareness.

Whatever it is, do it deliberately. Laugh in moments that might usually solicit a scowl from you, reach for a new thought in moments when you would usually confine yourself to resolve, believe in yourself more than you doubt yourself in a challenging moment, ask for assistance when you usually would not ...

Be!
Mary

We invite you to play a game today.

Every time you have a negative, critical, unkind, or diminishing thought ... take in a deep breath, smile at it, and replace it with Love.

Every time you have a worried, doubtful, dread-filled or anxious thought ... look right at it, remember possibility, and replace that old thought with belief.

Every time you have a controlling, disappointed, weary, or questioning (not to be confused with question-filled) thought ... release what you are clinging to, open your heart, and replace it with faith.

Every time you have a loving, generous, grateful or bliss-filled thought ... dive in, roll around in it, and pump up the volume!

Let's play then, shall we?
Mary

I t is a brand new day. All day long. You are a limitless being. What will you create?

Remember ... from the inside out.

Now you've got it goin' on!
Mary

B e loud about what you dream of, wish for, believe in. On the inside. Let it roar! Then give yourself to it. Again, on the inside. Remember, it is never really about the outside detail. It is about the spaces inside of you that you want to know more. Giving yourself to these spaces inside of you will draw to you their matches from the outside of you.

Ahhh, kismet,
Mary

We excitedly invite you to breathe life into yourself and your day. Literally, stimulate your thoughts, your emotions, your dreams, your consciousness, and your physical being by drawing your breath all the way up from your toes, letting it circle around at the top of your head, and then exhaling with great force back down and through. And, repeat ... anywhere, anytime.

Over and over. Get addicted.

More than you know,
Mary

E xercise your smile today. Give it a really good
workout. Your inner one and your outer one.
What is your inner one? The one that lives
inside you, just between your heart and your throat. When
you use it, it can cause you to grin or smirk just a bit and
spark the most wonderful glint of light into your eyes.

One and two and three and lift those corners,
Mary

Y ou know, when you agree to stretch your imagination, it becomes more flexible. This allows it to bend and twist and reach in ways never before experienced. The results are astounding. Today, consider what you have been imagining for your life and stretch it a bit further. Come on, reach! There, we knew you could do it!

Practice makes perfect. You can use your aspect of imagination in limitless ways. Choosing to do so will give you good practice for using it to manifest your desires.

Throughout your day today, consider using your imagination when you decide on the direction of your day, when you look into the eyes of another, when you look

into your own eyes in the mirror, when you hear something you do not agree with, when you hear something you do agree with, when you eat, when you think, when you play, when you converse ... you get the picture.

Stretch! That's it. Oh, and remember to attach your YES! Inhale and exhale.

Big love,
Mary

The thing is, happiness and doubt are choices. Much the same as deciding which socks to wear or which route to take to where you are going. Isn't it interesting that humans tend to believe that they have more control over the details (like socks and routes) than they do over what they think or how they feel? When in all truth, it is really the opposite. You see, it is how somebody thought and how somebody felt that created the socks and the routes for you to choose from in the first place. And, it is how you think and how you feel that influences your choice of what socks to wear or route to take—or dream to give permission to Now. Choose from the inside out: thoughts creating details instead of details creating thoughts. Much more powerful and exciting, don't you think?

Oodles,
Mary

There is a peculiar thing going on in your world: people are happy. There is strife, pain, illness, unfairness, and persecution and yet, people are happy. They laugh, they connect with one another, they find pleasure in simple things, they care, they love, they plan ... You see, no matter what is going on outside of you, inside of you there is always the knowing that happiness is your natural state and that there are far more things for you to offer happiness to than there are things to distract you from it.

Go ahead, throw a little happiness around today. See what it sticks to. Oh, and make sure to throw it at yourself first.

:) Skippity doo dah,
Mary

P.S. Spreading happiness is what will release the world from strife, pain, illness, unfairness, and persecution.

It is good to awaken to this day. This day that is brimming with possibility, promise and choices. What is your vision of you in this day? How will you show up for this day? What will you make yourself available to receive in this day? What will you choose to offer in this day? Ah, yes, how you answer these questions is indeed how conscious creation works. Now practice! :)

Streams of love,
Mary

Today is a good day for kindness. No matter what direction you throw it in, it will hit its mark. So go ahead and build it into your response system. Whatever comes before you today (including yourself), choose to live from your kindness in each moment. Now remember, we are not suggesting that you take things into your being this; we are suggesting that you put things out this way.

So if someone is being cross with you, it does not mean to be kind and take their crossness in; it means to observe that they are being cross and to choose to come from kindness in your response. Sometimes that would just be for you to smile, emote kindness vibrationally and walk away.

Oh, and you may want to give some quick "goodbye-see-you -later" hugs to frustration, irritation, blame, anger, ho-hum, terse, negativity, whining, judgment ... They don't hang around much when kindness is driving the bus.

Ta,ta,
Mary

sn't it interesting, that chances are, if a dear friend or loved one asked you to carry around an anvil, heaping, smelly laundry basket, or large hollow tube for the day or for the rest of your life you would at least question why it is necessary if not just completely refuse to begin with.

And yet, as we watch humans, we see that many are most likely willing to accept carrying around other people's burdens, complications, and vacancies just because they told you about them. Now there are two of you offering life to these things. And it doesn't stop there because now you are feeling the load of it all, so you tell others about it and they take it on and so on and so on and before you know it, the masses are weighted down. And you all wonder why you no longer know how to use your wings??

Try this, the next time somebody shares one of these things with you, instead of taking it on and carrying it around, nurturing and spreading its life, offer it love, peace and grace. These things can pierce and transform anything. Yes, even dirty, smelly laundry. Oh, we think we just saw one of your feathers on your wings puffing up ...

See you in the sky,
Mary

What is it that makes your life meaningful for you in this moment? You know, really meaningful. Take time to ponder this. Let it run through you as this day unfolds. As you experience each encounter, each exchange, each chosen usage of your time and thoughts - allow this pondering to be in the background observing, paying attention. You may learn something about yourself. Perhaps you will learn that your relationship with your compassion is what makes life meaningful to you. Or that your relationship with your curiosity or your intelligence or your love or your silliness is what sinks depth into your being.

Today, take a note card or piece of paper with you and as often as you choose to remember, record your observations of what makes life meaningful for you. Go ahead, release your hesitation and do this with zest. We bet you fill the page and ask for more paper.

Tra la la,
Mary

May we be direct with you? You are doing it all right. Yep, you are. Your thoughts, your actions, your beliefs - they are all perfectly aligned with your current vibration. You say what? You are not getting the results you want yet? Things are ok but could be better and you are a little perplexed or frustrated? How about you change where you are vibrating from and match your thoughts, actions and beliefs to your new vibration? Yes, that's it - now you've got it.

You see, if your current vibration is, "I'm working on creating the life of my desire ... the dream of me," then your thoughts, actions and beliefs will match that vibration. So, consider tweaking your vibration just a bit to, "I am creating the life of my desire ... the dream of me." Now your thoughts, actions, and beliefs will line up with that vibration. Can you feel the difference? We can.

Complete love,
Mary

79

You see, creating is just like making popcorn. You put the seeds (your budding of desire) in the oil (your thoughts) turn up the fire (your focusing of thoughts) and we let the seeds (your desires) rise up and burst into big, billowy kernels (manifestation of desire).

Just think, all these years you have been making popcorn and you had no idea it was reflecting the secret of creating.

Don't forget the butter (icing on the cake),
Mary

W hat decision will you make today? Will it be to believe in yourself? Or to reach for the stars? Or to live in the embrace of love? So many choices. Perhaps you will make a decision to move toward your dream or to take down a guard or to focus only on that which you want. (Not the wanting of it—instead focus on the actual thing or situation that you want—not on how to get it—just on the thing or situation. People get so confused about that.)

Whatever you decide, feel the power in your decision and let that power be the momentum that opens the gateway and sends you flying into and through the manifestation of the decision.

We will provide the GPS. You provide the fuel.

Toodles,
Mary

Greetings to you! Welcome to your new day. What will you do with it? What aspects will you choose as your companions to travel though it? Pick three. We realize this is a tall order to keep to just three, when there are so many possible combinations. And yet, we are still suggesting that you choose just three as your constant companions today. Write them down or carry three items in your pockets or somewhere else where you will be stimulated to remember them and make a very clear decision to encounter all situations and exchanges through these three aspects of you today. Now let's see ...

Curiosity, Imagination, Possibility ... or

Love, Compassion, Generosity ... or

Engaged, Alive, Revealing ... or

Innocence, Wonder, Flow ... or

Aggression, Frustration, Irritation ... or

Belief, Faith, Honor ... or

_____, _____, _____ ...

You fill in the blanks. Remember, it's not just a thought, it's a practice.

Juicy love,
Mary

t is a very important day today. It is a day of great celebration! A day of invention and possibility. All the reporters are lining up to speak with you. That is to say, every person you communicate with is listening to your every word (verbal and non-verbal). Many will take them in deeply and repeat them to others, spreading your essence, now mingled with theirs, throughout the land. What will you say as they all clamber to absorb the words and presence that you bring to this day? What will you choose to have reported about you to the masses of all that is physical and non-physical?

This is your day to be heard. Don't miss your opportunity to be clear, impassioned, and accurately reflected in your communications! Oh, yeah, tomorrow is going to be a great day filled with reporters, too! And the next day, and the next day, and the next day ...

Hip-hip hooray for unlimited opportunity!
Mary

P.S. This works when you are talking to yourself also. We know, we're watching, you do it all of the time.

I sn't it curious that tree branches easily and willingly bend when the wind blows through them and humans stay standing straight and firm and require the wind to go around them? That is unless we blow really, really hard and send you flying. You see, the tree branches know that the wind has something to offer them. It caresses their leaves and clears them of loose debris, nurturing their growth.

Today, be conscious of moving, shifting winds that are stimulated within you through your interactions with others. Consider lettering these winds ... change, new ideas, or different perceptions ... blow through you as you willingly bend to receive their gifts instead of meeting them with your firm resistance. Make yourself available for their potential offerings making room for growth and new life within you.

Light and breezy like a hurricane,
Mary

L ive yourself through the greatest experience of you. Consider what in this moment you love the most about you. Let that feeling percolate inside you and then respond to everything you experience outside you through this space of you. Remember not to pick and choose ... respond to everything this way.

Inspiring,

Mary

S o then, because you are an infinite, powerful, creating being, now remembering that you are the director of all that you experience within in your life, what's next? What will be your next thought? What will be your next decision? What will be your next offering ... your next releasing ... your next invitation? How willing are you to truly practice yourself in your most divine image of love, ease, abundance, healthy well-being, appreciation, peace, self-mastery ...? You see, your results will always be in direct measure to your deliberate practice. While it is possible to decide that you want to be love and then practice yourself through control, comparison, and jealousy, and eventually still experience yourself as love, the trip is not nearly as expedient or as pleasurable.

Live from your desired image of yourself now. In everything. Begin the practice of releasing thoughts and beliefs that are incongruent with it now. Become the student and the teacher of only that which matches your desire.

Always,
Mary

D o you ever just wake up ZESTY? We highly recommend it. You could choose cranky, tired, calm, drowsy, foggy, alert, startled, rested ... the choices are unlimited. And looking at it all from our perspective, we enthusiastically recommend you throw ZESTY into the mix. When you choose ZESTY you will move with a little ZIP in your step. Now, with ZIP in your step, instead of walking in your usual pattern or path, you will attract a little ZIG-ZAG into your rhythm of moving with life and in your way of thinking and creating—offering freshly turned fertile ground for new ideas and desires never before known to you. From this space, seek out delicious opportunities, conversations, and even cuisine that have a bit of ZING in them. Now your ZOOMING!

All you have to do to make this all happen, is to go to bed at night and catch a few ZZZZZZs.

Zowey!
Mary

R emember the saying, *When the going gets tough, the tough get going?* Well, don't you suppose the same theory could be used for, *When the going gets joyful, the Joyful get going"* or even better, *When the Joyful get going, the Joy gets going?* How about:

When the Peaceful get going, the Peace gets going ...

When the Graceful get going, the Grace gets going ...

When the Lovers get going, the Love gets going ...

Where will you choose to live from and get going today? So many choices! Be an instigator!

Riding on the stars,
Mary

What is it of life that fills you? What is it of you that fills life? That's the exchange you are here for you know. Pay attention to life today. And, in turn, let life pay attention to you. Take time to notice the nuances of how life caresses and adores you, how it is always reaching to know you better in as many ways as possible. And in perfect exchange, offer yourself to life by caressing, adoring and exploring it.

We think this could be the beginning of a beautiful relationship.

Just put your lips together and blow,
Mary

J– I don't think we need this PS ... it's not plagiarized.

P.S. What do you mean we just plagiarized? How do you know that we weren't the ones who gave them those words in the first place?

J ust for today, dare to ask thought provoking questions of those around you and then use your vibratory sensors to take in what is truly in and behind the resulting verbal response. What are your vibratory sensors you may ask? They are your energy readers. This is the space that when utilized powerfully, gives you complete insight and access to all understanding of creation. This is the space that cuts through illusion and experiences full truth - that which is real. It is important for you to practice this space because it is a key understanding in deliberate creation.

Practice feeling your conversations today. We do believe you will find it quite intriguing and expanding.

Full exposure,
Mary

After a while, anything repeated becomes habit, resulting in how you show up for life. That applies to your thoughts, your words, your actions, your beliefs, your desires, your rhythm with life. It applies to everything, even what you "expect" to happen. If you repeat "expecting to be happy," then you will be happy. If you repeat "expecting to run into a few bumps in the roads," well then, there will be a few bumps in the road. If you repeat "expecting to continually deal with adversity," you got it, there will be adversity.

To our amazement, we watch humans time after time practice or repeat your expecting of things not desired and being frustrated with how your life or at least parts of it are unfolding.

That's like putting your order in ahead of time, getting what you asked for, and then complaining about what you got. Or just quietly suffering while you eat it anyway. And then paying for it. Hmmmmmmmmmmm ...

Remember, repeat anything and you will become the habit of it. We suggest you ALWAYS order what is most delicious to you.

Pigging out,
Mary

Did you know that birds fly because they are birds and they have wings and they have been created as flyers? Oh, and that their parents push them out of their nest from high in the tree top and if they want to live beyond their first experience of touching the earth, they have to use their wings and believe in themselves as powerfully as their parents believed in them? Did you know that if the bird did not get pushed or leap from the nest that eventually, it would forget that it had wings and forget that it could fly and it would never know itself in its true vision?

Did you know that humans fly because they are humans and that they have wings (spirit) and they are created as flyers (engaged creators of life)? Oh and that their parents or friends or Spirit repeatedly push them out of their nest (comfort zones) from places and practices deep within them that they cannot imagine leaving and if they want to soar in life they have to use their wings (spirit) and believe in

themselves as powerfully as the one who believed in them? Did you know that if humans did not get pushed (nudged by loved ones) or leap on their own from the nest (comfort zone) that eventually, they would forget that they had wings (spirit) and forget that they could fly and they would never know themselves in their true vision?

So, what comfort zone are you willing to leap from or be nudged out of today so that you may experience yourself in your true vision?

Stretching and soaring,
Mary

Hello. Let's talk about BLISS, shall we?

Blessed

Loving

Imaginative

Savoring

Soaring

Sounds like a great place to live from doesn't it!

Today, practice yourself from this state of being. Know that you are blessed. Allow your gratitude for everything that you have celebrated, friendships, love, family, wisdom, adventure, yourself, experiences ... to rise up inside of you and kiss you on the cheek. Feel the loving nature of your

heart resonating through you caressing and stimulating every cell of your being. Play in your delicious imagination opening to all possibility of offering and receiving all that you desire in your experience. Take time to savor your moments throughout the day, being truly present and taking in deeply the gift they have to offer. And, release yourself to soar ... wide open, wings at full expanse, shields down, in the direction of your vision of yourself—your dream of you—well matched to the life you desire.

Uh, huh, got it going on ...
Mary

What makes your heart flutter? You know, what makes it skip a beat, sing out loud, blow wide open? When was the last time that you noticed? Today, live through your heart. Meet every moment, every conversation, every internal contemplation through it. See through it, listen through it, choose through it. Now, don't get living through your heart confused with living through your emotions. Living through the heart is pure, clear and direct. Living through the emotions, in some instances, is crowded, distracting and circumstance driven. That is until you have mastered living through your heart. Then you become the skilled, loving director of your emotions instead of the puppet mastered by them.

With great admiration,
Mary

Persistence. What are you persistent about? Really. What do you strive toward, move toward, believe in with abandon? Now, we are not talking about stubborn. Stubborn is something that you cling to and decide that you are not going to change your mind or your way about it not matter what. We are talking about true, unwavering persistence. Today, give much attention to that which you are persistent about that is congruent with your desire for your life. If your relationship with persistence has been neglected, have a recommitment ceremony with it and dive into rediscovering yourself in union with it. If you have never had a persistent relationship with anything then choose something - a vision, a desire, a dream of you - and make a commitment to a powerful, loving and constant relationship with it.

And, remember you are never ever alone. Ask for assistance where it is needed and then let it in.

You are getting so yummy,
Mary

Hey, let's play with a roundtable discussion today. Oh, come on, it will be great fun! We know, just to be interesting, let's make it one that is filled with only "Ds". You pick the subject or desire, then bring the following characters to the table to have an equally measured creation discussion about it.

Determined

Dedicated

Doubtful

Decisive

Deliberate

Diverse

Diligent

Delicious

Now, here are the guidelines - you sit at the roundtable in an equal seat with these characters and introduce the topic.

Maybe ... "I choose to be smarter, or to be one of complete well being, or more spiritually connected, or experiencing more freedom, or an excellent attractor of abundance ... " you see, the list could go on and on. Now, you give each "D" equal cadence or measure to express how it feels about the subject. The trick is in the "equal". Dedicated does not get more clout than Doubtful and Deliberate does not get more say then Delicious. And, yes, Doubtful is important to have at the table because it is real for you and giving it equal measure offers you the realization that it is not any bigger or more powerful than any of the other characters (aspects) that are real for you. This gives way for it's influence on you to lose its threatening, overwhelming status. Isn't that fun??

No cheating. Unless of course Diabolical is one of your "D" words.

Enjoy the game!

Mary

Sometimes, life feels nebulous, doesn't it? And sometimes it feels powerfully solid and directed by you. You are either seated somewhere on the bus watching the scenery or you are in the driver's seat of the vehicle that you specifically chose and decisively selected all of the options for. Both have their benefits when you are engaged for the ride.

So, what will you choose as your mode of transportation today? Will you be sitting back, paying attention to the vastness and diversity of the scenery, gathering information and contemplating your piece in the Big Picture, or will you be wearing your leather driving gloves, mapping a specific route, and driving full speed ahead toward your destination?

And we haven't even started talking about planes, trains, and spaceships yet ... So many choices.

Travel well,
Mary

Happy Day! Happy, happy Day! Yes, that's it ... Happy Day. Just a suggestion.

With passion,
Mary

P.S. Yes, it really is that simple—and it is in your hands ... and your toes ... and your laugh muscles ... and your fingertips ... and your choosing ... and your deliberateness ... and your knee caps ... and your birth right ... and your whistling ... and your love ... and your ... Get it?

Today, pick a dream, any dream. Spend five minutes embodying the essence of it as early in the day as you can offer time to it. Perhaps now. Or now. Ok, then throughout the rest of the day, pay attention to your thoughts, actions, choices, decisions, interactions, responses, etc. Notice all the times you spend in any way that is incongruent with your dream.

For example, you may say, "My dream is to be fit, slim and healthy." Then you spend the majority of your time thinking you are overweight or out of shape and achy. (thoughts) When you have free time, you always choose to do something sedentary. (actions) You always choose the donut over the carrot. (choices) You continuously decide to start "working on it" tomorrow instead of today. (decisions) When you converse with others you talk about how hard it is to find the time or the energy or the will get into shape. (interactions) When an opportunity arises to do something that will move you in the direction of your dream, you find excuses to not do it. (responses) ... Acting in a way that is consistently incongruent with your dream may mean that

your dream is created from a "should" or somebody else's vision of you. Or it may mean that you do not believe in it. Or it may mean that you don't believe in dreams coming true.

If you find that you are constantly incongruent with your dream, take a trip inside and see what motivated the dream in the first place. Make sure it is your dream of you. If it is, then make some very clear decisions about what is more important to you: holding onto doubt in your dream or holding onto belief in it. If belief becomes the vision that you channel yourself through as you move toward your dream, you will find yourself becoming much more consistent in your congruency with your dream. If doubt remains the key element, then incongruent will remain a steadfast partner in your creation.

And remember, you can't fool yourself. So talking gibberish or merely offering lip service to yourself will not get you far. Believe, believe, believe ... it's worth it.

Squishy hugs and deep belief in your dreams,
Mary

Dreams and sparkles and crystals and shiny things ... what is their allure for you? Or is it contemplation and green fields, and smooth, deep waters that you have an affinity for? Perhaps both?

The point is, your world is full of people (sparkly, shiny ones and smooth, deep ones), things, and experiences that attract you for a myriad of reasons. Today, pay attention to what is attractive to you and make note of it. At the end of the day, write a story of you in association with what you noticed to be attractive: that which stirs you, or enlivens you, or deliciously stimulates your birthing of desire or that which brings you peace and love and joy. Or that which offers drama, chaos, concern, intrigue ... Be truthful with yourself in the recognition of what attracts you.

This practice will bring you much awareness. And, if you choose not to do it ... well, that will bring you much awareness also. One practice will bring you awareness of what drives and feeds your dreams, the other will bring you awareness of your resistance to move toward them. It's all creation. :)

We'll leave a light on for you,
Mary

P.S. Remember ... the story is about you in association with what is attractive to you ...

Sometimes, life throws you a curve. You know why? Because somewhere in you, you were desiring another way to experience it. And the only reason it may frazzle you for even a moment is because you have temporarily forgotten that you are an infinite being, with access to all possibility, capable of handling anything that comes your way with ease and grace and maybe even exuberance. You see, curves are thrown to remind you of who you really are.

Remember to lean a little for the inside curves.

Love,

Mary

So, what's new? What new thought or new response or new receiving space or new offering are you willing to embody today? Did you know that even the slightest change in trajectory will completely change the outcome of a bullet hitting its target? If you have been aiming for something and are not quite hitting it yet, then pick a new thought, action, belief ... even if only slightly different.

Be sure to make the change one that is moving in the direction of your desire, though. We certainly don't need bullets flying backward or sideways. That creates all kinds of havoc. Either that or make the target bigger ... You know, for instance, change the desire from, "I want a convertible." to "I want to experience my life in a way that allows me to feel the wind blowing through my hair as I move full-speed ahead in the feeling of complete freedom and adventure." Get the picture?

YUMMY,
Mary

Consider this: your life is in your hands. Will you treat it with loving care and nurturing or with recklessness and neglect? It's your life ... in your hands. Will you give it your undivided attention or ignore its calling out to you? It's your life ... in your hands. Will you be at peace with it or in a constant state of conflict? Perhaps your current practice is to mix it up a bit ... love it, neglect it, nurture it, deny it, honor it, push against it ...

Today, focus on treating your life in a manner that feels good and lends itself to the dream of you more than you focus on treating your life in a way that doesn't.

Now that is living,
Mary

It is a popular belief that humanity is basically good. It is also a popular belief that there are tricksters and bandits and "losers" everywhere, ready to pounce on unsuspecting victims.

Hmmmm, which belief best matches your dream of your life? Both beliefs have accuracies. Which one will you match your vibration to today? Go ahead, take charge and pick one and then pay attention to how your outside world reflects your inside world today.

Oh, this is going to be juicy!
Mary

Hint: Pick "basically good" and then feel free to exaggerate and believe that humanity is basically spectacular ... There, now you are on track ... it's just a suggestion. :)

ip, hip hooray! It's a brand-new, skippidy do dah day! You know what that means? It's your choice. Get it? What today becomes for you is your choice. Will you invite a new experience? Will you create some calm and comfortable familiarity? Whatever you choose ... remember, you have to show up for it in a vibration that can experience it that way.

You see, if you invite a new experience and show up for the day looking through eyes and heart that believe it will be the "same ole, same ole" then, well, all kinds of new things or opportunities can show up and you won't even see them. So, it's like this ... "Today, I desire brand new, so I choose to show up brand new." Or, "Today, I desire calm and comfortable familiarity, so I choose to show up calmly with a comfortable familiarity with myself."

Whatever you choose. Oh, and then show up for ...

Getting jiggy with it,
Mary

G o ahead, play with the dream of you. We know it is something you deem as very special and of great value, something to maybe be worn on only very special occasions ... Go ahead though, play with it. It is not as fragile as you may think. Actually, it is pretty durable and even unbreakable, this dream of you. Get your hands on it, take it around the block, run with it ...

No more waiting.

Your dream of you is not something that lives in the distance, somewhere out there just beyond reach. It is right there inside of you, wishing to be expressed and practiced daily—not to be put somewhere safe and unused. So today, to whatever degree you choose ... LIVE IT!

Believe now,
Mary

L ive literally today. Define and be exacting about the dream which you are deliberately designing in your life.

Whatever you are desiring, literally climb inside it and live it out loud. Like this: consider the desire; allow the sensation of it to come to life within you; delve into it vibrationally with all that you are; and radiate the resulting embodiment of it throughout your day.

Now you are literally becoming your dream.

Riding the wave of loving you,
Mary

I t's a beautiful world. It really is. Yes, this is true. As a matter of fact, it is so full of beauty that it would be overwhelming for you to attempt to truly absorb all the beauty it offers in every moment. Yep, it wouldn't take long at all for you to hit your saturation point and then to savor the experience of it and then to give yourself pause to let it all soak in deeply feeding and nurturing your inner world in splendid ways. And, all you have to do to experience this is to pay attention, be available and receive … easy.

Oh, yeah, and to remember that you are beauty to assure you feel its match.

You and the world … lovely couple,
Mary

Write yourself a love song. Make it meaningful and true. At least write the refrain. Like this:

I'm falling in love with you more and more every day.
I want to know you in every way.
When I think of you, I feel all of the riches inside of me.
Gets me excited about what we are going to be.

And the beat goes on,
Mary

Yep, we're snapping our fingers together now ...

Today, forgive yourself for something, anything. Doesn't matter what you choose. Just reach inside, pull up forgiveness, and envelop whatever you choose within you with it. Perhaps an old regret or a new one. Perhaps an incongruence in your belief and action in relationship to your desire. Perhaps your practiced inability to truly forgive yourself.

Whatever you choose, make it real. After you have done it once, love yourself more and do it again. Go ahead and spread your aspect of chosen forgiveness around a bit, flowing over ancient history and current events within you.

You see, the fun thing about this is, if you are remembering that you are a vibrational being, then after the initial launch, you don't have to make it about the story of where forgiveness has been missing, dredging up the old uncomfortable feelings associated with it. You just simply agree that today, you are going to live in the vibration of forgiveness of self for everything that you have been harboring "against" yourself and release you back to you in love.

Vibration rocks,
Mary

Find a penny, pick it up,
All the day, you'll have good luck.

Do you believe it? It only works if you believe it. You see, your belief is what gives you your focus. What you focus on is what you experience. So, if you believe you will have good luck, then what you focus on and experience in everything, in every moment, is your good luck.

Works the same for belief in love, friendship, ease, peace, abundance, joy, self-mastery, healthy well-being ... On the other hand, it also works the same for belief in struggle, doubt, betrayal, loneliness ... YOU Choose :)

What will you focus your belief on today?? We suggest you select any and everything that allows you to experience the dream of you to any degree.

Pennies from heaven,
Mary

Right now, there are grand forces utilizing divine creativity to bring together a multitude of opportunities, situations, and details that will perfectly match your current vibrational attractors.

What are "vibrational attractors," you ask? Your thoughts, your actions, your beliefs, your decisions, the aspects you live from ...

Give us something yummy to play with, won't you?

Tantalizing,
Mary

What is it that sparks your heart? You know, what really gets you juicing? What are you truly attracted to that feeds this space?

We asked you about your heart. Why are you using your head to find the answer? Today, ask your heart to make evident that which is a match to it. There's no judger in there, you see, just pure, clear wisdom and knowing of you.

Match. Not a Match.

Match. Not a Match ...

Open,
Mary

P.S. When your heart gives you evidence of what is a match, consider giving yourself permission to open to it. Just a suggestion ...

Dream. With your eyes wide open. All of them!
Enchant your world from the inside out.

With a touch of splendor,
Mary

Blend your love into your joy, your joy into your wonder, your wonder into your inward wisdom, your inward wisdom into your outward expression, and offer yourself to the world.

Or just skip, sing, dance, and puddle-jump. Or ... whatever else you choose.

Infinite,
Mary

Sing the song of your soul today. In other words, tell only the truth. Begin with telling yourself the truth about you first. Let us help you get started:

The truth is, I am love.
The truth is, I get scared sometimes.
The truth is, I believe in ...

And continue.

You are sooooo beautiful! (and that's the truth),
Mary

Drift into the abyss of freedom today. Free your thoughts. Free your heart. Free your dreaming.

Fly,
Mary

Make this a seed-planting day. Offer little nuggets of your wisdom to conversations with yourself and with others. Cultivate and care for the ones you give yourself. Release attachment to the ones you give to others.

Oh, and, don't confuse wisdom with opinion. There is a vast difference.

Joyfully gliding in your wind,
Mary

Leap, skip, jump, dance, zeal, reel, feel, be, glee, climb a tree, set yourself free. Make this a day of emancipation from hesitation ... playing small ... settling and excuses.

Dive into yourself and pull out your amazing light and remembering of who you truly are and live you out loud today! If you are catching your breath just a bit at the thought of actually doing it, just begin with five minutes and grow from there. You WILL want more!

Come on, put your toe in!
Mary

Make it a window day. You know, how you can look through a window seeing beyond the glass even though it appears to be a solid surface. Encounter life, people, conversations, new awareness, desires, and yourself this way today. Then, if you feel so inclined, open the window and climb in (or out).

Windows are a great example of edgelessness. While it may appear that they separate you from what is on the other side, they really don't at all. Looking out or looking in.

Love without limits,
Mary

Pay attention to what influences you. And why. When you are in the beginning, middle, or end of doing something, note what or whose influence prompted you to choose to do it. If it was somebody other than yourself, consider that person and what qualities he or she possesses that you respond to that are part of the shiftings and moldings of your life. Your influences.

Like this: I am so inspired by my parent, friend, mentor ... to be courageous and dive into difficult situations with complete belief that I will be safe and all will turn out well.

or

I am so tortured with living my life through the aspects of obligation and fear that my parent, friend, mentor ... taught me.

or

I am so ignited by the passion and gratitude that fill my soul and my heart naturally from the center of my existence and drive me to offer myself to my life and the world purely and completely.

There are many "influence fuel" options. What are you filling your tank with?

Vroom, vroom,
Mary

We invite you to take a moment to center and bring up the image and vibration of a shooting star. Feel its magnificence, its "wheeeeee," its magic, its granting of one thousand times on one thousand wishes as it glides across the sky. And know, truly know, that, that star is a perfect reflection of you.

Wowed by you,
Mary

Ride the wave of change today. Release resistance and zoom along the deliberate, offering edge of expanding, shifting, and becoming. Let movement be the fuel that catapults you into the center of experiencing your desired creations.

Brakes off. No skid marks in you today.

Let 'er rip!
Mary

Believe. Open. Breathe. Invite. Imagine. Release. And ... Fly! Fly!

With all our might,
Mary

What will you fill yourself with today? What thoughts will you spend your time with? What imaginings will you expand? What delectable spaces of love will you open to? What passions will you race with as you express your truest essence?

Good thing you know you are edgeless so you recognize that your ability to fill is infinite. There is always room for more.

Yes, yes!
Mary

Be a lion today. Let your roar out. You know, that extraordinarily, perfectly pitched, pulsating vibration that lets the world know who you are. Why waste yourself on anything else?

Pulsing love,
Mary

Have a GREAT day today!

A glorious ... radiant ... excited ... anticipating ... tantalizing day!

And tomorrow... a ground-breaking ... rip-roaring ... enthusiastically expanding ... awe-inspiring ... totally titillating day!

And continue ...

Passionately yours,
Mary

What an incredible day to wake up to! One with YOU in it!

Oh what, oh what will you do with it?!

Maybe you will consider inviting "thrill" to be your guide? Or "serene"? Or "curiosity"? Or _____? You fill in the blank. There are infinite choices and you are in the driver's seat!

Kowabunga, baby!
Mary

ctively and excitedly search your heart. Go ahead. Explore all of its corners, echoes, and pulsing. Let it offer you the recognition of your unique and perfect loving through its infinite wisdom. And then let that be the beacon through which you shine yourself into the world today.

Once again basking in your glow,
Mary

Dream from the center of your heart.

Love from the center of your soul.

Imagine from the center of your spirit.

Anticipate from the center of your body.

Activate from the center of your mind.

Today ... Live expressly from the center of your perfect union.

Beautiful creation!
Mary

What is the pulsing in you? The pulsing that never dims, never fades, never relinquishes you? You may cover it, muffle its volume, and ignore it with some success, and yet, it is always still there waiting, ready, and completely available to you.

Is it passion, peace, visioning, love, curiosity, non-complacency, illumination ...? Pay attention to your natural pulsing today, and set yourself free to know and live your true essence out loud—internally and externally.

With grand passion and love,
Mary

P ractice fullness today. Eat until you are full, laugh until you are full, love until you are full, learn until you are full, breathe until you are full, inspire until you are full, receive until you are full ... You get the idea.

What will you choose to fill yourself up with today? Because, you know, you could worry until you are full, fear until you are full, doubt until you are full ... That would be silly, though, wouldn't it?

Remember to consume what you desire to chew on and expand from.

We particularly enjoy the yummy, filling taste of love, Mary

A re you doing it yet? Are you offering your dream, your passion, your wonder, your magic, your splendor, your desired creation to yourself and the world? No matter what your answer is, consider offering more of it today than you did yesterday and more tomorrow than you do today and continue and continue and continue.

Delight and delight and delight.

Be YOU,
Mary

L aunch something new today. A new idea, a new hope, a new permission, and new belief, a new curiosity, imagining, adventure, desire, flight pattern, story, dream, relationship, interest, exploration, discovery, way of loving ... And remember to climb in and take yourself along as its constant and ecstatic travel companion.

Providing the fuel for mach speed,
Mary

It's all right here, right now. Everything you dream of, everything you vision. You created it when you imagined it. Now, open up and let it in and let yourself out into the world embodying it! Feel how your belief in your desired life swirls through you, lighting up all of your spaces of renewal and invention. Let your soul sing today.

Breathing you,
Mary

How will you share your innate wisdom with yourself and others today?

How will you offer it through your actions, your words, and your presence?

By the way, wisdom never comes with force and instead always comes accompanied by calm knowing without agenda. Makes it easy to distinguish from opinion which does always come with force and agenda.

Right there in the center of you,
Mary

Notice one thousand things to be grateful about today. Sound like a tall order? It's not. Allow the essence of your gratitude to rise its immensity in you and you will not be able to keep up with the countless moments, experiences, things, exchanges, and passions that offer you ample and abundant opportunities to know the power and magic of gratitude.

No matter what is going on outside of you, when you meet it with gratitude—your gratitude—you will know possibility there.

Shining in, through, and along side you,
Mary

B e a force to be reckoned with. A force of love, a force of peace, a force of joy, a force of inspiration, wisdom, innocence, curiosity, honor, playfulness, insight, integrity, wonder, trust ... Now those are beneficial ways to use force!

Remember, there is a big difference between *being a force* and *forcing* something. The former offers expansion (love); the latter offers squashing and condensing (control).

In awe of your brilliant light,
Mary

Consider keeping a grin on your face and a spark in your eyes today. For the WHOLE day. Not just for five minutes or five hours or when something evokes it in you. The WHOLE day. Invite the world to meet you square on through your grin and your spark.

Ohhhhhhh, juicy, juicy, juicy!
Mary

B e astounding today. Oh, and, while you are at it, be astounded also.

Emanate aliveness and full engagement.

Be the current,
Mary

A re you listening? Go ahead. Take a moment to stop rushing. Breathe yourself into stillness. Ok, there you go. Now you are listening.

You have everything you need to create the life of your dreams right there inside of you. Are you still listening? Good. All you need to do to reveal it all to you is to love yourself into believing in you—or believe yourself into loving you, completely and powerfully enough to set everything within you free to serve you.

Ahhhhhh, take the plunge,
Mary

Yes! YES! YES!" Go ahead, say it and feel it just like that. Over and over.

YOWSA! Doesn't that feel GOOD? We encourage you to do a lot of it today. As often as possible, turn on your "Yes." Give it to yourself and to others with great generosity. Spend it like you will never run out, because you won't. Actually, the more you spend your "yes," the more you will have.

Works that way with love, too ... and peace ... and joy ... and wonder ...

Passionately yours,
Mary

C reate harmony today. Seek out ways to blend yourself in peaceful union with others and/or with nature. Recognize yourself where you are in the oneness in association with other people or nature, instead of where you are in separation.

What is your matching space? It doesn't have to be anything big ... when it comes to another person, it could be that you both have hair on your knuckles or when it comes to nature, it could be that you and a blade of grass both feel the wind when it touches you.

Consider giving more particles to allowing instead of rejection or resistance today. Feel the harmony that is available to you in your world and let it in.

In oneness,
Mary

L eave fingerprints today. Touch the world with you.

Continuous love,
Mary

Act on your dreams today. In whatever way and to whatever measure you believe you can. Do something, anything, to lean toward them or leap right into the middle of them.

Here are some ways to get there:

- μ Be your own biggest influence.
- μ Engage your eagerness.
- μ Let go of your excuses.
- μ Offer plentiful particles of belief and decision to them.
- μ Validate yourself as worthy.
- μ Expand your belief in possibility.
- μ Grant yourself permission.
- μ Respond to life through appreciation.
- μ Obliterate all temptation of "can't."
- μ Witness and stimulate your YES.
- μ Initiate and live in the state of invitation.
- μ Nurture your passion.
- μ Give yourself to your dreams.

Into the forever with you,
Mary

Spill some wonder today. Drench your world with it. You have more than enough to share.

Remember to soak yourself first. Yep, YOU, right there, at the front of the line again. Good job!

Delighted to know you,
Mary

Grab today with gusto!

Grand
Utilization
Stimulating
Titillating
Outcomes!

It is your day, after all. Use it wisely.

Welcoming

Insight

Seeking

Expansion

Loving

You!

Oh, how we could go on ...

Good on ya, mate,

Mary

perate from "Open" today. Open mind, open heart, open doors …

Soar,
Mary

Love uncontrollably today. Let 'er rip! Exude the movement of love in all of your moments. And then, pump it up some more. Resist temptation to alter or dim this activity when you face contrast, adversity or challenge. That is when you will want to use it the most.

Remember to reach inward and outward with it simultaneously.

Launching,
Mary

What brings you joy? Yes, we know that is kind of a trick question.

There is only one answer: YOU. Now, how about this? What inspires, enriches, expands, ignites, augments, enlivens ... your joy? Every moment you encounter, if you meet it through your joy.

Works the same with every aspect: love, fear, curiosity, possibility, limitation, worry, delight, wonder, mistrust, passion ... You decide.

Mix it up a bit. Use them all! Then hang out the most with the ones you like the best.

Admiring your puzzle,
Mary

Look inside today. Notice your own infinity. Infinite thought, connectivity, belief, choices, creativity, love, curiosity, imagination, desire, decision ...

Create from the inside out.

You've got us wrapped around your finger,
Mary

Oh, and infinite charm. Don't forget your infinite charm.

How will you honor yourself today, and therefore honor the world? How will you treasure and embrace the truth and beauty of your own heart? Your deeply committed-to passions? Your splendid in-motion creating? Answer: You will do it all by choosing.

What are you doing now? Answer: Choosing

And now? Answer: Choosing

What will you choose to spend yourself on today?

On the edge of our seats,
Mary

Did you know that life is a pure, flowing stream packed with opportunity, thrill, adventure, wonder, forecasting, deliberate choices, zoomy possibility, tremendous love, unfathomable riches, embracing friendship, unimaginable splendor, excitable passions, peace filled pathways, open doors, giants, flying, freedom, expansion, constant moments of birthing, brand new ecstasy inducing creations and MORE?

LIVE!!!!

Whew,
Mary

The thing is, you are right in the middle of possibility all of the time. So, when you are tossing up your "possibility balls" (thoughts that you create from), remember to mostly catch and "swallow" the ones that truly nourish you, not the ones that just fill you up.

Oh, and be honest with yourself about what you have been filling yourself up with. "I'll have a plate of drama with a side of anger topped with disbelief and mistrust. Oh, and for dessert, I will have some yummy cynicism, smothered in creating from the outside in ..."

Or, "I'll have a plate of opening and expansion in awareness with a side of excitement topped with trust in myself and the universe. Oh, and for dessert, I will have some yummy belief smothered in creativity ..."

What's on your plate???

We always start with a heaping portion of love and then select yummy sides that compliment its deliciousness completely.

Oh, and for dessert, infinite embracing of you, every time.
Mary

When things feel like they are spinning out of control, just hit the pause button. Close your eyes, and breathe deliciously slow, elongated breaths into your mind until it calms and you remember who you are (love) and why you are alive (love).

Regain yourself there, and then pull that breath all the way down to your toes and repeat until you begin to feel the stability of the return of you to you. Welcome yourself back with a warm embrace. Open your heart and your eyes and move forward.

Anywhere, anytime,
Mary

Love your moments today. Inside and out.

When you are feeling disgruntled, dismayed, disconnected, disastrous, it is because sometimes, you just simply forget to love.

Turn it on and leave it on. Offer and receive every other aspect through it. Go ahead. Just give it a try.

Shining on and in you,
Mary

D o something important today. Think a thought that inspires you. Take an action that invests in you. Release a boundary that limits you. Make a choice that enhances you. Open an internal space that expands you. Invite an opportunity that stimulates you ...

And, pass it on and on and on.

Echoing your love,
Mary

Today, listen. Open up and truly receive. Today, pay attention. Be present, alert and fervently engaged in awareness of your moments, your exchanges, your opportunities expanding.

Today, love without edges. Reach. Dive. Offer. Receive. Begin. Expand. Endeavor. Open.

Becoming Oneness,
Mary

Did you know that while you are brushing your teeth, driving your car, walking through your living room, eating your dinner, laughing with your friends, reading your books, shopping for food, standing in the elevator, washing your hands, doing your job, hugging your loved ones ... we are stimulating all of the particles of the Universe to move into formation to be a perfect match to your most extraordinary imagination of yourself?

Imagine BIG!

Edgeless,
Mary

As you move through your day, in every moment, in every breath, in every thought, let yourself hear the roaring whisper that lies, always ready, in the background of every particle of your existence ... "Love is the answer."

Quenched by you,
Mary

Let the awareness of all things moving in perfection be with you today. Because they are. Let the ease of life be what gets your attention, unless of course, you are in the mood for something else. Whatever suits you today, put it on and wear it well.

You are looking snazzy in that outfit,
Mary

What do you admire in everything and every moment you encounter? There is always something upon which you can use your aspect of admiration. It really cranks your inner light voltage up when you choose to turn it on, so ... how about it? Are you willing to admire something about all things and all moments today?

We are and we have started with you.

More than you know,
Mary

What will you allow to seep into your experience today? Love, curiosity, enjoyment, trust, willingness ...?

Consider being porous. All it takes is one drop to start a stream.

Our love,
Mary

Take a moment to breathe into your heart center. To take lots of moments to breathe into your heart center. What will you choose to inhale? What will you offer in your exhale? Will it be the same with each breath or will you mix it up a bit?

The combinations are infinite and you can do it anywhere, anytime, one breath at a time or lots of them in a row. No special place or circumstance required. Perhaps the best things in life are free.

Floating on your rhythm,
Mary

L eap. Reach. Dream. Trust. Embrace. Ignite. Live.

And repeat ... over and over and over ... only if you choose to and you are ready, of course.

Always right there with you,
Mary

You are a miracle. Isn't that fun to know?! Yep, little ole you, a miracle. All those particles, guided by your will, constantly forming and reforming, leaning this way and that way, creating a life never before known in your internal or external world, moment to moment, day to day, week to week ...

We are on the edgelessness of our seats, anticipating the millions of never-before-experienced creations that you will offer to yourself and to the world today.

Marveling at your creativity and generosity,
Mary

O ur love for you is beyond your current ability to measure. And, we know everything about you. What will you do today to allow your love for yourself to catch up to our love for you?

Psssst ... You might want to begin with releasing judgment utilizing your aspect of love. Many attempt to release judgment through their aspects of guilt, should, force, negativity, and even judgment—that really doesn't work so well. Use your love. Move toward all of your aspects, all of you, all that exist in your world through love. Judgment, self-recrimination, fear, or disconnection just really won't stand a chance.

Unshakable,
Mary

P.S. When you are ready, throw a little bit of belief, wonder, hopefulness, delight, embracing, and trust into the mix. There you go ... now you are beginning to catch up to us.

Goooood DAY to you! Open your heart, mind, spirit and soul. Take a deep breath and dive into something important to you. Saturate in it. Ignite in it. Revel in it. Even if only for five minutes, say "yes" and give it to yourself and the world.

It is important to us to love you with all that we are. Is it important to you to let it in?

Abundantly,
Mary

Do you ever notice when you gaze up into the night sky, sometimes the stars seem brighter, sometimes still, sometimes twinkling, sometimes dimmer, and sometimes they are completely covered by a cloud so you can't see them at all and yet you know they are there burning, living, being brilliant?

That's how it is when we look at all of you.

Thank you,
Mary

Thank you. Thank you for your choosing to live, expand, dream, love, offer, become, engage, solicit, breathe, imagine, reach, drench, whisper, shout, stir, launch, rest, invent, thrill, appreciate, anticipate, receive, fly, be, play, learn, teach, rise, slip, create, begin again, believe ...

Thank you.

Eternal gratitude,
Mary

Today is a day for dreaming. Pull out your imagination, your limitless potential, and your "Yes" and DREAM you and your life in vivid, living color.

Remember to do it with feeling and commitment.

Beaming and inspired,
Mary

Your individuality is showing. Your ability to see things from a different angle … to engage yourself with others from a unique perspective … to create your uncommon life out of thin air. Very impressive. Like a book we have never read before.

What a page-turner!

Chapter by chapter, line by line, we love you,
Mary

ook to the grandness of the sky today. Let it be your indicator of absolute, infinity, and grace. Always there. Always more. Always offering and receiving.

Do you suppose your heart learned how to be a heart by observing the sky or do you suppose the sky learned how to be the sky by observing your heart?

Either way, when the grandness of the human heart is matched with the grandness of the sky, magic happens.

Make wishes,
Mary

Allow. Yep, that's it. Allow. Resistance is futile.

Warming the cockles of your heart,
Mary

It is in the midst of change that humans identify spaces of themselves, before unknown to them, and expand. This is what stimulates you to constantly create change: the desire to know the self in new and yet unexperienced ways.

Without change, you would just go through life, day after day, moment after moment, repeating yourself. Leaving little exact carbon copies of you all over the place in your trail.

With change, you color your world with "brand new" consistently and constantly. Inspiring new possibility, new awareness, new ideas, new hope, new insight, new depth, new love, new thought, new creation ... So the next time somebody asks you, "What's new?" say, "Me!"

Take your flight jacket,
Mary

E mbody the wind today. Feel yourself as you move through every space of your choices and resulting experiences as the wind. Caressing and therefore gaining intimate familiarity with everything you touch along the way.

Now, be sure to pay attention as you move through your day. Are you a gentle summer breeze; a lingering, swirling wind that stirs the leaves in a circular pattern; or gale-force hurricane winds? Perhaps a mixture of them all in varying moments. Just remember the wind you choose to embody determines the kind of impact you leave in your path.

Stirring the winds of change,
Mary

Dive in. No hesitation. No excuses.

Double dog dare you,
Mary

B e bold. Tell it like it is. Express yourself clearly. Let the thunder inside be heard. Speak your truth as you believe it, without agenda. Latch onto the transformation energies swirling around you and release yourself to them. Become who you are, more today than yesterday. Believe in you with all your might.

Adding fuel to the fire,
Mary

I t is simple really. Don't you see? Nature reflects human and human reflects nature—completely. Life is life. Blend your life together with nature and you will have immediate, intimate understanding of limitlessness.

You are as big as the sky and as singular as a blade of grass.

Live in union,
Mary

What are you attracted to? What are the magnets in your world that pull you with great force? What part of you is responding to them? Pay attention. Notice if what you are attracted to is pulling on something in you from where you have been in the past, where you are in the present, or where you desire to go in the future.

Riding the wave of creation,
Mary

W hat is the gift within you that is desiring to be unwrapped today? You have so many of them—some already with ribbons pulled, lid open and moving now within you fully celebrated; some like "ladies in waiting" lined up, primped to the max, vying for your attention, wanting to be picked; and others tucked away for whatever reason, off in the distance, patient in their lingering until you seek them out and bring them to the surface.

Just choose one ... or two ... or ...

You deserve them. They were made just for you, after all, Mary

What is "living in a state of excellence" for you? Find your answer to this question and actively live it out loud today.

We'll be in the cheering section,
Mary

P.S. "I don't know" is not an allowable answer ...

When you color a picture, do you stay inside the lines? Perhaps you are one who outlines the picture before coloring it in to establish an even more vivid line to aid you in staying inside the lines so the result is neat and crisp? Or, perhaps you are one who shoots over the line here and there or all over the place and adds additional items to the pre-drawn page? Then again, maybe you are one who always finds pre-drawn pages too confining and chooses a blank page to create on.

How are you coloring yourself into your world? Are you neat and crisp, staying within the prescribed lines, or do you cross the line here and there or all over the place—adding your own twist to that which is prescribed?

Or, are you unconfined by anything prescribed, creating that which has never been thought of before?

We would bet you are a bit of all of them. It's not about being one or the other; it's about blending all of the colors and styles that you are, cohesively and joyfully, so you always feel the flow of your creation.

Using the deluxe set of crayons with extra colors and a sharpener,
Mary

Let yourself completely consume this day. Gather all its riches as you go and open to receiving them deeply and fully with all your heart, all your soul, all your mind—all your particles open for the blending. You, immersing your whole self into your experiences, choosing always in the direction of your desires.

Stirring the mix,
Mary

F abulous day, don't you think? Oh, we do. We do indeed. This day is open and ready for you to fill it with whatever you desire. What will you give to it? What will you offer? Your love, your imagination, your delight, your belief ...???

Go ahead. Choose and spill into this day. If you do not get back what you desire right away ... give more. Practice ...

Dancing in the magic of you,
Mary

We invite you to focus on beauty today. It is so infinitely abundant when you open your eyes. All of them ...

The eyes of your soul, the eyes of your mind, the eyes of your heart ... you get the picture. Live through all of your eyes today, so you may truly see.

Enchanted with you in every moment,
Mary

I t is time to undo your knots. You know, the thoughts, beliefs, resentments, defenses ... the spaces you hide inside yourself, hoping nobody will see or know about that you cling to, even though they leave you stagnant instead of flowing.

Pay attention to these things as they arise, greet them with full-out love and then tell yourself the truth about what choosing to stay in companionship with them is doing to you. You see, your role is just to tell yourself the truth. The truth will do the work to undo the knot.

Oh, and no placating yourself with excuses. Nice try though.

Twinkling,
Mary

T oday, let innocence and curiosity be your guides. Yes, we said guides, not companions. Call them up from within and let them lead the way.

Practice yourself through them. Get to know them. They will serve you well.

Oh, this is going to be juicy,
Mary

Jump, leap, bound, hop, skip, soar. With elation. Every time, every time.

At your side,
Mary

We suggest that you choose an "in spite of" day today.

Love, in spite of ...

Trust, in spite of ...

Move toward, in spite of ...

Believe, in spite of ...

You know, step into who you truly are and desire to be in spite of all the excuses—clearly "justified" excuses, we understand—and yet, still excuses.

Shining light from every angle,
Mary

One thing for you to remember in every moment, every breath, is that you have wings. Use them. Quit looking for the instruction manual and just use them. You already know how.

Nice loop de loop,
Mary

Abracadabra! Poof! There you have it. Go ahead, use your magic wands and transform away! They are right there within you: the power of choice, the power of will, the power of YES, the power of permission, imagination, love, possibility, cleverness, belief, commitment, dedication, unwavering consistency, rejoicing, gratitude, awe, innocence, curiosity ...

Just remember, your wands are only effective on you. Stop waving them at other people and outside experiences. Use them to transform yourself and attract new or additional others and experiences that match the transformed you.

Firing up the rockets so we can keep up with you,
Mary

Today, put your hesitation on alert. Let it know that your mantra for the day is, "Look out. Here I come!"

Ripping open the express flow for this one,
Mary

Where do you suppose dreams spend their time when you are not hanging out with them? In the Big Dream Waiting Room in the sky, that's where. Hang out with your dreams today. They have been waiting long enough.

We have got to get some better magazines in here,
Mary

Today, imagine yourself there. A lot! Dress for it, inside and out. Look through the eyes of it, inside and out. Receive through the feeling of it, inside and out.

What "there" are we referring to, you ask? You choose.

Saturating in Love,
Mary

W hat are you willing to transform with just a moment's notice? You may find this a peculiar question and yet what we know is that you can only shift, in a moment's notice, those things to which you hold no resistance.

Opportunities often come with just a moment's notice. Are you ready??

Loving all of your particles,
Mary

G rab hold of your steering wheel, choose a direction, and drive, drive, drive. Don't waste one precious drop of your fuel detouring to places that do not support your destination. And for goodness' sake, pay attention to the "dead end" signs. We watch so many of you say, "Well, it doesn't look like a dead end. I'm going to try it and see." If the sign is there, loud and clear, just know that even though you can't see the end of the road, it is indeed there if you take that direction.

Loving you clearly,
Mary

When you are getting ready to go someplace today, even if it is just to the kitchen to grab a snack, take your dreams with you. Not in a bag you carry along with you—you could misplace that or maybe even consider it a burden to carry around all of the time.

Instead, carry them within you by letting them have life in every particle of you in every moment. There. Now you're looking good.

Big smooches,
Mary

Allow your eyes to know what your heart is seeing. We notice, quite often, that humans do it the other way around. They let their hearts know what their eyes are seeing. You see, the vision from the heart (through love and wisdom) is always much clearer—even when the vision from the eyes is 20/20.

Through and through,
Mary

Y ou know it's all just a matter of TIME—Total Imagination Managing Eternity ... Or Titillating Inspiration Magnifying Everything. Or Transforming Internally Mastering Ease.

Go ahead. You come up with some translations. Whatever suits you. Now you are getting a taste of self-mastery. You decide what everything means and how you use it—even TIME.

Whispering sweet nothings in your ear,
Mary

E njoyable day to you. Oh, yes. Pleasurable day to you. No, that's not quite it … Oh, this is it: Extraordinary, multi-dimensional, ease-filled, joy-embarking, love-expanding, soul-soaring, mind-blowing, Life-choosing, toe-dancing, truth-exploring, spirit-flying, bliss-soaked day to you!

There, we believe we got to it with that one! Whew! Now, take that into your day and live from the center of your most extraordinary vision of your life. Because this day is ripe for the picking.

It's Harvest Time,
Mary

P.S. Just for fun, greet somebody, anybody, with at least one of our wishes for you today. For instance: "Good mind-blowing morning to you, Boss!" "Good soul-soaring morning to you, Co—worker!" "Good toe-dancing morning to you, Spouse/Lover!" You get the picture …

What is the nature of your song? You know, the personal rhythm that lives within your being. Is it jazzy or contemporary, pop or rap? Perhaps your song croons to a country sound or blasts through you like screaming rock-and-roll. Oh, maybe you are of the easy-listening variety or is it the plucking of the strings of a banjo with a bit of folk that we hear coming from you? And, there are always the long, deep, soulful blues, or the high-pitched, erratic movement of techno, or the primitive, stirring sounds of native drumming and ancient wind instruments.

Whatever it is, listen for the nature of your personal song today. Take time to feel your personal rhythm as it moves through you.

Music is an excellent way to experience and understand vibration. Go ahead, experiment. Listen to a variety of it. Feel its rhythm and allow the "match" to soak in or the "not a match" to move right past you to catch the beings it belongs to. Once you discover the "matches," explore their nature. Discover why they move in rhythm with you. Feel yourself vibrationally as them, and know yourself better.

You might even consider writing a little something down about it, like, "I am Soulful Blues because ..." or "I am Easy Listening love songs because ..." or "I am Techno because ..."

Putting on our dancing shoes,
Mary

P.S. Don't forget Big Band, opera, acoustic, Swing, Indie ...

We find it marvelous that humans fly all the time without even noticing. That's right. You do it. What do you think daydreaming is? It's flight. Sometimes with a flight plan registered and sometimes just taking off with no destination or duration in mind. Isn't that fun! We are great proponents of daydreaming. We suggest you do a lot of it. We suggest you fill all of your spare moments with it. Much more productive than worrying, stressing, fretting, analyzing, revisiting regrets ... Wouldn't you agree?

So, go ahead, fit some daydreaming in today. And don't forget the fuel (vision, belief, permission) that helps them come true.

Get your head back in the clouds,
Mary

The challenging thing about limitlessness is that it comes with everything. It's not even served on the side. It's right there on everything on your plate. Whether it's love, fear, ease, excuses, peace, victim-hood, joy ...

The fun thing is that you get to decide how much to eat. You see, it's all about portion control. Taste test all of it. Fill up on the stuff that tastes good to you and remember if what's on your plate doesn't look appetizing to you, you can always clear your plate and start over.

Lighting the candles on the table,
Mary

Today is a day of complete truth. Well, actually, every day is. Yep, it's true. Every day is a day of complete truth.

Today is an opportunity for you to pay attention to when you embrace truth, when you avoid it, when you put a bend on it, when you run it through a filter and it gets a bit murky, when you rejoice in it, when you twist it, when you deny it, when you color it a bit ...

Go ahead, practice feeling the truth. Use your wisdom center (your heart). Use your power center (your gut). These are the most accurate centers for feeling your vibrational detectors of truth.

Your mind, while acting as a wonderful asset to you for storing the information about truth once it is experienced, is not your most pure way to identify it. That is because the mind will take you through the memories and stored information of everywhere you have been, therefore basing your experience on what you have experienced before and not on what you are experiencing in the moment.

By the way, we are talking about the truth within you. You need to get squared away there before you can truly even begin to recognize what is true in the world around you.

Stimulating your future,
Mary

How about you skip today. You know, speed up your pace a bit, lift off the ground a little, and bolt forward springing off of one foot and landing squarely on the other and repeat. We dare you. While it would be great fun for you to do this physically, bringing back innocent moments of childhood, we are actually suggesting that you do it internally. Pick any desire that you have been putting on the shelf and activate it by applying the principles of skipping: Speed your pace with it (give it your undivided attention). Lift it off the ground a bit (energize it with your passion for it). Spring forward (do something to activate it). Land squarely (feel the solidness of your desire), and repeat (keep up the momentum) It's up to you. Whatever you choose.

Nudge, nudge,
Mary

L   et's decide today. Decide on a direction, an attitude, a desire. We say, "Let's" because we will be right there with you. We love to play in "Decision Vibration"! So let's decide on something, anything today— large or small, important or silly. Decision Vibration comes with the aspect of self-ownership and you know that self-ownership is always stimulating to self-mastery. So anything you do with Decision Vibration will take you directly along the path of self-mastery.

If you don't want to pick something or just can't decide what to decide then instead, pay attention to the decisions you make every day already. Note where you make them internally: what to wear, what to eat, what direction to take, what to say, what to think, what to feel, what to believe ... you get the picture. Oh, joy, joy, joy! We get to play in Decision Vibration with you today! Happy Day, Happy Day!

Riding shotgun,
Mary

Today, open yourself to the mystical. Let yourself run free and dance and play with mystery, innocence, possibility, joy ... See with your thousand eyes. Inhale and exhale in union with the Universe as it breathes you in the remembering of no separation. Listen with your wholeness, allowing the rhythm of sound to drink you in as you swirl with its beauty. Ah, yes, OPEN.

Savoring,
Mary

Welcome to this new day. It is well prepared and ready for you. Everything you need is in it. Utilize it well. Oh, and remember that what you experience in it is what you are reflecting to it.

In other words ... If you show up worried, you will mostly experience things to worry about. If you show up joyous, you will mostly experience things to be joyous about. If you show up loving, you will mostly experience things to be loving about. This is because you experience everything through the "moment-to-moment-practiced" you ...

Today, be aware of how you are practicing *you* in various moments throughout the day by noticing what you are experiencing. Or, choose now what your predominant practice of self will be throughout the day and be aware of how you experience your various moments differently through this space of Self.

We pick groovy,
Mary

It is an amazing day to be alive! Yes, this day is packed FULL of opportunities for your "Yes's" and "I am willing's." How will you choose to employ your Yes's and Willingness today? Come on … put them to work for you … offer them overtime! The riches they produce in your life will be well worth the investment.

Worshiping you from afar,
Mary

Today, replace every habit-produced resistance with the vibration of "I open." Replace every spark point of negativity with the vibration of "I open"... before you open your mouth to express the judgment. Replace the active irritation and frustration within you with the vibration of "I open." Replace doubt, bewilderment and confusion with the vibration of "I open." Replace disappointment and fear with the vibration of "I open."

In other words ... PRACTICE the vibration of "I open" today. Go ahead. Just try it and see what ideas, spaces of imagination, new avenues of thought, gained understanding, activated expansion, unlimited possibility, this vibration opens you to. Are you willing to meet life through "open" today? Are you "Open for Business"?

Opening doors,
Mary

It's sometimes a challenge to practice the self in a way that is congruent with your vision of yourself, isn't it now? Actually, sometimes it takes great effort and determined commitment. Oh, and ... letting go of all of those excuses as to why it isn't so easy ... now that's a challenge. Good thing you are up for it. Good thing you have everything you need right there within you to rise to the challenge. Good thing you have open access to everything that you are and unlimited assistance from all that is physical and non-physical. Good thing you believe in your vision and your vision believes in you ... Oh, did you know that part? Your vision believes in you.

So do we,
Mary

Do you ever feel stumped? You know, truly baffled ... completely perplexed ... We are not talking about confused, puzzled, or unsure. We are talking about downright mystified. You do? GOOD!

That means you are choosing to live your life to its fullest. No stone unturned. No avenue unexplored. We suggest you live your life in a way that runs you square into "stumped" as often as you can. And when you are there ... remember that it is not a roadblock, it is just a road yet uninvented waiting for your direction. Anywhere. Your roads can lead anywhere. You just need to gather the materials (remember who you are and what you are capable of), create the design (choose a direction) and build (believe in yourself). Oh, and hire a construction crew (physical and non-physical assistants) to help you. Do remember to interview well. Only those who believe in, support, and enhance you need apply.

Brick by brick,
Mary

Pure pleasure to you on this day. Yes, pure pleasure. You deserve it. How will you allow it to find you?

Will you be easily found, showing up in a way that it can offer itself to you in every thing, every space, every exchange? Or are you more of a "sneak up on me" kind of person, needing it to jump out from behind a tree or around a corner to surprise you here and there throughout the day? You decide. We suggest you put a brightly lit, profoundly gargantuan, energetic arrow right above your head with the words, "Here I am, Pleasure. Come and get me!" posted on it. You know, only if you want to.

Stirring the magic potion,
Mary

Today, let's dive in, shall we? Into the delicious underbelly of your self-existence. What is it that moves in your center ... nudging, stirring, whispering, wrestling, flying itself into your awareness when given permission by you? What of yourself wants, begs for, and sometimes demands more of you? Can you feel it rising? If not, sit a minute and let yourself feel its tantalizing invitation to allow it more life in your life. Then free yourself to let this stirring of your self-existence, the space that believes in you relentlessly, rise to meet you with its passionate embrace. Full of all of its possibility and movement and guidance to take you directly into the center of realizing the dream of you.

How do you free yourself, you ask??? Release resistance. All of it.

Eradicating the straightjackets,
Mary

Today is an offering day. Yep, glad we were able to tell you. Would have been such a blunder for you not to have known. So go forth and offer.

Offer your listening where it is needed. Offer your insight (not to be confused with opinion) where it is requested. Offer your wisdom where it is inspired. Offer your permission where it need be granted. Offer your love with glorious, infinite abandon. Oh, and remember it all starts with you. Go ahead deliciously saturate yourself. Then move onto others from that state of being.

Now you're cooking,
Mary

Even in its "bleakest" moments, life force flows. It may "feel" like a tiny trickle, and yet, it is still flowing. Isn't that amazing? The sheer determination of your life to move with and through you. Always, constant, relentless, every moment ... dedicated completely to you. And clever. Oh, so clever. Just when you think the dribble is not enough to sustain you, that dribble penetrates something in you, and a new opening appears and expanse comes in and with time and decision, the "feeling" of the full on rushing stream of your life returns.

Bravo!
Mary

oday is a day to dance in a field of daisies. What is that, you say? You can't find a field of daisies. Well, then, dance in the knowing that you are a splendid, remarkable, loving, beautiful, delicious human being. That is the field of you that we dance in every day.

Loving you,
Mary

ake arrangements to laugh today. What? You say you can't make arrangements for that? Laughter just comes naturally, spontaneously because of who you are and what you attract to you. Hmmmm, so does everything else. So does everything else.

Open.

Yours always,
Mary

"Life is all possibility."

"Life is limited."

You choose.

If you are feeling "stuck" on how to tap into the "all possibility" choice, back up your lens to get a broader view of your life. "Stuck" usually comes from looking too closely at one particular aspect of your life for too long from the same angle.

Camera's rolling! ACTION!
Mary

Today, practice more love than doubt. More peace than confusion. More joy than resentment. More risk than reservation.

Remember: within you first and then let it out.

Streams, waves and floods,
Mary

Ask yourself this. What is my dream of a lifetime? Really spend some time in the feeling and the image of your answer. Script it if you would like. Then, define your role. What parts of this dream are completely determined from the inside of you—nondependent on people, places, or things outside of you. And, begin, NOW, playing your role exquisitely.

Go ahead! Wear the costumes that match your role ...

Filling the audience for you,
Mary

If you had an owner's manual—you know, an instructional "how to" booklet for you—to hand out to others, what would it have in it? How would your components be broken out and labeled in the diagram? What would be the key elements of description on "how to care for" or how to "troubleshoot" for repair?

Necessary tools in hand,
Mary

Perhaps today is a good day to fly. Perhaps it is a good day to open your heart wide. Perhaps it is even a good day to believe in yourself and your dreams so deeply that you never forget how to again.

Choose,
Mary

There is a miracle around the corner. And, there is a miracle right there inside of you—brimming with hope that you will let it be known and shared with the world. It is you.

So the question is: do you live for the miracle around the corner or do you live the miracle within?

Sprinkling magic dust into your nooks and crannies,
Mary

Hint: You can pick more than one.

I t is our observation that when it comes to creating, many people are very clever and diverse, and yet, often limited by their current thought pool. Today, we challenge you to add a new thought, a new awareness, a new opening to so much more, to your creating juices. And tomorrow do the same and the day after that and the day after that ... and on some days, add two or three or twenty—seven new thoughts, awarenesses, and openings.

Now you're cooking with gas,
Mary

Tip: New thoughts are not created in the mind alone.

It is with the drive of pure determination, utter commitment, and catalyzing belief that humans wholly and successfully offer themselves to a desired creation. Either that, or you stumble upon it while you distract yourself with something else that feels good.

Oh, happy, *HAPPY* day,
Mary

f you only had 1,000 thoughts to use today, what would you think about? If you only had 1,000 words to use today, what would you choose to say?

Oozing with anticipation,
Mary

Have you ever wondered why caterpillars are willing to go through the cocoon process to become butterflies? They simply can't deny themselves of knowing what's on the inside bursting to come out ...

What are you willing to do to allow the bursting inside to find its birth, its flight?

Basking in perfect love for you,
Mary

et out to do five things today. Five important things like: deeply love, ecstatically celebrate, truly listen ... you get the picture. Leave "forgetting" in the slumber you rose from and remember to feed yourself with what is important today.

Soooooooooo delicious!
Mary

R evel in the juiciness of possibility today! Really offer yourself to it. No matter what you encounter, chant your mantra, "I give myself to possibility today!" And, smile, smile, smile!

Oh, and leave the monotone energy behind—it is such a downer for your flying spirit.

Blistering hot, ignited Love!
Mary

E manate gratitude today!

Yep ... Emanate, emanate, emanate gratitude today. Even if it's just for the fact that you have nose hair, or that flowers bloom and birds sing and people love. Whatever you can find any sense of gratitude for, tap into that and flow.

Ahhhhhhhhhhhh, thank YOU!
Mary

Knock one out of the ball park today. Get into a perfect stance (know what you want), keep your eye on the ball (commit to your focus), line up your vision (align yourself with your desire), and swing with all your might (give yourself completely to it).

Get out of the stands and onto the plate.

Cheering for you,
Mary

Ooze significance today. Free yourself to notice, take in, and embrace what is truly significant in your moments. Internally and externally. What blends and what stands out?

Noticing what you notice,
Mary

Let life love you today. Let it grab you and whisk you away into its edgeless landscape and limitless attractions. Let it weave all of its possibility and belief in itself right through all traces of your limiting resistance and open you to the pinnacle of experience of you and then fuel you for more of all you celebrate.

Sweet, savoring, fully charged Love,
Mary

Each new day, each new hour, each new moment brings opportunity for life experienced like never before.

Will you create your new moments through old ways or through new possibilities? So much to imagine!

Infinite,
Mary

Carry a feather with you today. An actual feather, or a picture of one, or simply the word written down on paper. Let it serve as a reminder to you that you have flight in you, and you can use it to speed you, glide you, soar you into the center of your dreams.

Fueling your wings,
Mary

Bask in your own brilliant light today. Really open up to its glow and its warm embrace and sink in. Let it wrap you in its complete knowing of you from the center of your existence. Let yourself collapse into its wonder and live from there.

Now that's divine,
Mary

t's a big, big life. Packed full of opportunities, choices, possibility, and there is no external instruction manual. However, there is your internal guidance system. Keep it open. It is amazing to us how many people go through so much of their lives without consciously and decidedly creating themselves through the use of it.

Tap into your internal guidance system today. Let it take you to who you are visiting your Earth to be.

Offering Light to your path,
Mary

Breathe deeply several times today. Go ahead. Inhale all the way down to your toes, hold it, hold it, hold it, and release. Now with intention. Breathe in love, wonder, and richness. Let your breath fill every particle of you it can reach. Hold it, hold it ... and release, blowing out all of your stagnant energy, all of your old, unwilling spaces. Your old stories that don't fit you anymore. Your regrets. Your grudges. And repeat and repeat and repeat. Ahhhhhhhhhhhhhhhhhhhhhhhhh...

Talk about a speedy way to lose ten pounds or at least feel completely lighter.

Loving you powerfully,
Mary

"Come into my web," said the spider to the fly.

What webs of thought is your inner spider (captor) luring your inner fly (innocence) into? Old, tangled spaces of entrapment that no longer match you and your desire for flight and speeding vibration? Perhaps it is time to use your thousand eyes to see the webs and buzz right past them into the continuous voyage of your new creation.

Buzzing innocence—try it on!

Zzzz, zzzz,
Mary

Today let your spirit fly untethered. Go ahead, set it and you completely free to soar. Exploring and discovering through innocence and complete love—opening you to MORE. How? Close your eyes, center, and let yourself feel its-life opening force igniting within you. And then, encounter everything through this space of complete, joyous abandon.

Enjoying your company,
Mary

Love someone today. We mean really, really love that person. Offer the other your time, your open heart, your undivided attention, your belief, your willingness to truly know the other and embrace the other powerfully and expansively.

Did we mention that it will be very important for you to be loving yourself this way to truly be able to offer it to another? Yes, always start at home, right there in the center of you.

Before, during, and after,
Mary

Explore within today. Notice, be intrigued by, and explore who you are in all of your spaces. You are a truly remarkable person. Spend time with you. Get to know you. Allow yourself to be consumed by your own beauty and then share it with the world. Let it flow.

Deliciously sinking in with you in Love,
Mary

Look for what matches today. Especially in the moments that feel most contrary. Open to recognizing where you do connect, what you can understand, how you can love and allow intentionally with your nature when not always naturally with your personality. Open to recognition, connection, and possibility. Expand.

Doors wide open,
Mary

Persistence. Persistence. Not with frustration and doubt. Instead, with passion and belief. Giggles and exuberance. Calm and focus. You know the way.

Believing in you,
Mary

Yes, you have both wings and weights within you. Which do you choose to use today? You see, it all really is your choice. Isn't that exciting? You in charge all of the time!

What? You say, "Not really"? Too much to always be the one leading the way. You would like to relax a bit and release all of the responsibility? Hmmm, well then, we suppose you just chose wings.

Relax and glide, relax and glide.

Catching thermals by your side,
Mary

B egin and end your moments with applause today.
You can do this internally or right out loud.
Either way, really offer yourself the sheer
exhilaration of your essence of THRILLED as you move in
union with your day. Let it rise up in you and blast out
through the palms of your hands ecstatically coming
together in complete celebration of all that you encounter.
Let life excite you! Let you excite life! Feel the thrill!

Rockets flying in all directions!
Mary

Welcome to this brand new day! What will you aspire to today? To open, to be peace, to engage in connection with others, to activate your belief in your dreams, to find moments of pure magic, to release yourself to unstoppable laughter ... to forgive? Soooooooooooooooo MUCH to choose from. Enjoy your day.

Yes, you can have it all,
Mary

Our vision of you, our dear, is bigger than you can imagine in most of your moments. We are speaking of our recognition of the greatness that you are, the potential that you will rise to, the new avenues to life and love and fulfillment, yet uninvented, that live within you.

Go ahead, play in your imagination today. You know, feed the possibility of you. Ah, yes, offer nourishment where it is needed.

Overindulging gain,
Mary

Love is all there is. Remember that in all of your interactions and presented opportunities today. When you feel challenged, remember yourself as love. When you feel resistance, remember yourself as love. When you feel unsure, remember yourself as love. Oh, and, do revel in the deliciousness of all of Love's closest friends, like possibility, joy, elegance, dreaming, kindness, open, ease, well-being, infinity, peace, offering, delight ... You get the picture.

Smile pretty now,
Mary

D id you know that your life would move along much more smoothly, you would reach your goals so much faster, and consistent peace and serenity would be yours if you would just cooperate with yourself. Yep, it is true. No excuses.

No whining. Just pure cooperation. That's the big secret. The key to the palace of pure life. Question is ... will you do it?

Behind you all the way,
Mary

How will you occupy your time, your thoughts, and your creation space today? What will you activate of yourself to invigorate your dreams? What aspects of you will you invite to your roundtable to create and implement the plan for your path to manifestation of your desires? We bet you had no idea how busy you would be today, consciously and actively creating from the inside out, did you? Now get on it! You have much to do. No wasting your time on what is not working or what feels complicated, or what (or who) you judge to be wrong—you have done enough of that.

Dancing in the light of your creation,
Mary

Today, be conscious of living your day on a continuum. Feel how each experience impacts the next. Whether you wake up sluggish and then stub your toe, or you wake up energized and then sing in the shower ... pay attention to how your vibration moves with you from one moment into the next. Also pay attention to how your vibration shifts or remains the same when challenges or triumphs arise.

Question: "Mary, my whole day was going so great. I woke up happy, I danced in the shower, traffic was a breeze, my productivity at work flowed flawlessly, I was connecting with people around me in fun and meaningful ways, and then ...

... I got a call from a loved one who is really struggling and it all vanished. I began to worry, I felt irritated and hope-less. How could I create that when I was in the middle of consciously creating a beautiful day?"

Answer: "When the challenge occurred, you changed your vibration. You stopped believing and began doubting. Very different vibration indeed."

No excuses. No whining. Choose.

Swimming in the Sea of Vibration,
Mary

oday, practice, practice, practice telling yourself the truth. Access your resistance as an ally in this process, using it to stave off the temptation to analyze, justify, blame, or make excuses. This will leave you clear to live yourself from the inside out and celebrate the knowing of what is the truth of who you are, how you believe, what you feel—these spaces have great impact on the outcome of your creations ... Just tell yourself the truth and from that space of inner connectivity, tell yourself the truth about what the truth is for you and then choose. Choose. Now remember, this is the truth about you, not about what you perceive of things or people outside of you. Instead it is about the truth of how you vibrationally respond to everything inside and outside of you—real or imagined.

Just is,
Mary

Your internal landscape is full of mysteries, isn't it? These mysteries give way to lots of self-explorative questions like: Why do I feel this way? Why do I sometimes delve incessantly into my desires and why do I sometimes seem to forget that I have them? Why do I feel confident in one moment and lost in the next? Why do I have a passionate response to some things and a repulsive response to others? Pay attention to your "Why's" today. And then do not seek the answer to them outside of you. Instead, remember that you hold all of the answers to all that you seek to know, right there, inside of you. Sometimes you just have to look behind the barriers of "No, I don'ts" and "I don't knows" to find them. Being willing to do this and then acting is a tremendous step in your achievement of self-mastery.

Whenever you are ready,
Mary

P.S. Remember, you have full access to everything you have ever encountered, experienced, and explored to assist you in your seeking of self-knowledge.

L aughter is a wonderful thing, don't you think? We are talking rip-roaring, belly-jiggling, knee-slapping laughter. It releases tension, offers joy, inspires freedom, and invites oodles and oodles of vibrational flow. Get in the stream. Open yourself to love through laughter today. Even if it's just a chortle, giggle, or big grin that puts those cute little creases by the sides of your eyes—open and enjoy!

Soaking in it,
Mary

Are you willing to be brave enough to be vulnerable today? Defenses down, opinions at bay, resistance dwindling, the need to be right on hiatus. Are you willing to make yourself available to love in friendships, in intimacies, in all of life through what is real instead of what is filtered by past experiences or mistrust? All kinds of love. The wide open spaces of it, the deep intricacies and purity of it, the twists and turns and heart expanding vibration of it. Love is everywhere and in everything. Are you willing to be vulnerable so you can experience the lion's share of it today and always?

Roaring loudly,
Mary

L et's play a game today, shall we? The objective of the game is to consume all the love, possibility, imagination, strength, playfulness, bliss, insight, curiosity, and vision that is available to you in every single breath you take, and then pass it on. Tag, you're it!

Running free,
Mary

L et's make this a day of gratitude. Yep, a day of the glass not only half full but flowing over. That's right, a day of full recognition of the gift, the potential, the possibility in every moment. A day that meets your heart wide open and actively offers love to every thing and every person and every experience you encounter. A day, like any other, only with the slight adjustment of absolute, unlimited, far-reaching, life-expanding, soul-satisfying, spirit-freeing GRATITUDE.

YUM!
Mary

Today, "respond in" instead of "react to" your day and all of the moments in it. Your response system is internal and uniquely designed by the truth of who you really are. Utilizing this space of you will profoundly offer you to yourself and to the world in pure reflection of what really matters to you—love, connection, truth, expression, authenticity, playfulness ...

The interesting thing is, a great majority of humans live more frequently from their reaction system, which really has very little to do with who they really are and much more to do with what is going on around them. Therefore, they experience very little of their true selves day after day after day. It must get distressing to be so far away from home (your true self) with such frequency.

Fluffing the pillows for your homecoming,
Mary

What is it that inspires you? In knock-your-socks-off ways and in whispering, subtle ways. What thoughts, contemplations, observations, or stimulations spur and stir you into movement within? And in these moments of inspiration, what story do you tell yourself? Is it a story filled with affirming belief and direction and launching? Or is it a story of lack of time, lack of resources, lack of belief? Decide. From the library of all of the stories that have been written and are being written right now.

We've got our reading glasses on,
Mary

P.S. Your story has infinite and delicious potential. We are hanging on every word as it is written.

How is it that you come to conclusions? Or shall we say, how is it that you come to your beliefs? Are you a gatherer of new information, opening up and reaching out to pull in concepts and ideas and things that until this moment were unknown to you, to stir in together with what you already have within you, to reach an expanded understanding resulting in a new or shifted belief kind of bloke? Or are you a sure and steady, "this is what I believe because it is what I have always believed it" kind of bloke? Likely, you are a bit of each, depending on the belief and how you came to it to begin with.

Today, we invite you to pay attention to what you allow expanse to in your beliefs and what you become immovable on in your beliefs. This awareness will offer you great insights into yourself. Ahhhh ... yet another step in self-mastery.

Get ready, set, GO!
Mary

W hat will you choose to carry with you today?
What will you take along into all of your
moments? Will it be your love, your insistence,
your disgruntledness, your humor ... ? Can you feel the
difference in the weight of the vibrations of the words? Go
ahead make a list of all of the aspects that you are feeling
right now ... intrigue, doubt, desire, hope, resistance ...
Now read them and feel the weight of each one. For
instance, you may write down Love or Vision and experience that while they may be huge, they possess no weightiness at all, they actually remove weight instead. Now, you
might write down Resistance or Doubt, which may possess
a similar size of hugeness; however, they may feel crushing
in their weightiness. So, considering this, we ask you again,
what will you choose to carry with you today?

Sending wings for your shoes and love to guide the way,
Mary

There is a rhythm to everything. Allow yourself to be still for a moment, close your eyes, release yourself to the inner spaces. .. Now begin to tune into your awareness of the pulsing—the vibration of silence moving in rhythm with sound. From this space, feel your energy, your silence, and your sound ... as they move in conjunction with all of the silence and sounds around you. Open yourself to feeling the connectivity of all things coming together in perfect rhythm. Oh, you may have to release resistance to experience the purity of the rhythm. It's worth it!

Swaying to the music,
Mary

P.S. You are everything you encounter. Therefore, finding your rhythm with all you encounter will create much more flow than resistance will ever even touch the edge of.

Today, be honest. Yep, that's it. Make that your main focus for the day. Think you can do it? Did we mention we mean internally? Be honest with yourself about your thoughts, your beliefs, your choices, your decisions, your opinions, your contemplations, your words, your love, your actions ... Remember, we are talking about within—about yourself. No coloring or bending or contorting the edges to make things fit tidily into your judgment of what you want to believe about yourself or what you think you "should" be thinking, feeling, being ... Just tell yourself the truth about yourself in every arena (without judgment to the degree that you are capable of it) and then, when you are ready, choose. "This stays. This goes. This I will box and shelf for awhile until I can know it more clearly ... "

Be thorough,
Mary

It is your brilliance that lights the path of a thousand directions, a million possibilities, a billion choices, a trillion experiences. Yes, you read it right ... YOUR brilliance. Your shining light that illuminates your way. When you lose your way, it is just that you have temporarily forgotten that it is YOUR light, YOUR brilliance that enlightens your perfect knowing of how to proceed and you are attempting to use the light of another instead of your own. That other's light may offer welcome insight and guidance that will assist you with expanding your own brilliance, but in the end and the middle and the beginning, it is always your light that offers you the grandest clarity in your own experience of you.

Let's light the world together,
Mary

Make it a smooth sailing day today. Want to know how? Just simply decide. Remember, it is not about how life shows up for you; it is about how you show up for life.

Choosing ease and satisfaction,
Mary

P.S. We've got our Kool Kat sunglasses on. How about you?

sn't it amazing that the stars are always in the sky, the sun always rises, and the roots of trees always grow firmly into the earth. These are things you can count on. When all else seems topsy-turvy, these truths are constant. You can use them as anchors. Something solid to lean on when you need a break.

On the other hand, isn't it equally amazing that the number of stars in the sky constantly changes, the sun while rising every day offers varying distances from the earth, and the roots of trees are constantly choosing new routes and paths to grow.

So even within the constant, there are variances, birthing moments, and the possibility of new direction. These are also things you can count on. When all else seems topsy-turvy, these truths are constant.

You can use them as a catalyst. Something to look to for direction when you open and offer yourself flight. Ah, humans a reflection of nature once again.

Stretching our roots while creating our flight pattern,
Mary

Quite a powerful thing, the human heart space. Vast in its capacity to open and grandly flow love, grace, and forgiveness. Fierce in its capacity to catapultingly express passion. And, astonishing in its ability to acquiesce to your internal direction and close or withdraw itself in part or in completeness. Hmmm, remember when you activate the latter, your heart space closes off to you in equal measure to what or to whom you intended to close it off to. Same thing goes for grandly flowing and catapultingly expressing ... what you offer to others is what you are simultaneously offering to yourself.

Every time,
Mary

Often times, you hit the nail right on the head. You know what you know and you move with it. Your heart opens and with the gale-force winds of change, you shift your life by choosing your dream of you above all else. Make today one of those times.

Thoughts, decision, action ... ROLLING!
Mary

Did you ever stop to think? Or are you more of a "start to think" kind of person? "I was moving right along when I stopped to think ... ""I was moving right along when I started thinking ... "Hmmmm...

Bathing in curiosity,
Mary

Hey, consider letting today be a day of ooozzzing appreciation for being alive! Live through thoughts like, "Golly-gee willikers, my body is a wonderful and amazing plaything—especially my toes and my belly button and the backs of my knees and my ears and the place behind my ears—oh, and my eyelids … " Or, perhaps you prefer to do it by breathing in deeply, closing your eyes and allowing the celebration energy of your soul in union with your spirit to rise and expand and fill the entirety of your being with remembering all of the possibility that exist in every breath you take, in every miniscule moment of life, your life, and set yourself free to embrace and experience your moments from a truly attentive and present space of yourself. Go ahead, try it. Show up today in the FULL-ON richness that you are.

Meet you in infinity,
Mary

You are the original pattern of love.

Contemplate that.

More than you know,
Mary

P.S. What could possibly be more valuable?

L et us take you on a trip to the stars today. The stars of your internal universe. Yes, you have them ... sparkling and glowing and filling all of your senses with the most titillating tickings of magic and pleasure and bursts of laughter. Let it be revealed to you the patterns of all of your internal points of light that emanate from you when you set yourself free to be shared with others in oh-so-poignant ways. Patterns of love and grace and wonder. Look to your inner starlit sky today. Notice your own constellations and the forms they take.

> *Twinkle, twinkle, little stars,*
> *How we wonder at what you are ...*"

For you,
Mary

All worry aside today, decide on something and love it with all your might. We suggest you choose something in your internal environment.

Oh, what to choose? What to choose?

Internally yours,
Mary

Are you willing to make today an adventure? If so, will it be an adventure of the heart, the mind, the soul, the body, the spirit ... ? Go ahead, invite up your essence of adventure and live yourself through it today. Internally and externally ... leap, bound, prance, jump, dive, release ...

Oh, we love it when you crank up your juice!

Swinging from the stars,
Mary

Take a look at life from the inside out today. Yes, consciously dedicate your whole day to this practice. Your inside. Not anybody else's. Yours. Really notice how you see things from your inside premium box seat. What aspects can you feel instantly joining you in this very special seating section as you consider your view? What is your view from the inside? What aspect filters does your observation of life come through?

Do you see life through judgment, allowing, whimsy, seriousness, expansiveness, hesitation, wisdom, joy, love, harshness, worry, innocence … ? In what moments? Who do you hang around with the most? How does the internal company you keep impact your choices your creation your belief about what you are seeing, experiencing in the outside environment? Yes, you are powerful, very powerful indeed.

Loving you wholly,
Mary

R espect ...

Rather Extraordinary Shared Purpose Eliciting Conscious Trust.

Who, where, what do you respect? Is it mutual? Mutual is important.

Creating vast playgrounds for you,
Mary

Today is a day for blowing bubbles. Truly, reach into your innocence and blow gently. Watch the magic of tens of hundreds of bubbles appear from one tiny circle of glinting soap film. Now, really, come on ... reach joyfully into your innocence and believe that something that appears to be small and perhaps insignificant (the glimmer of possibility) can become so magical when you blow your breath (belief) into it gently without force. Now you've got it.

Kisses to your forehead,
Mary

Hike your inner landscape today. Put on the shoes you best like to walk in and set out. Explore all of the wide, open spaces and the narrow, squeeze-your-tummy-in-to-get-through-them spaces. Stand on the edges and look out at the horizon. Use your wings to carry you to the really, really high places and your soft landing gear to lilt you gently into the canyons. Pay attention to where there are treacherous, jagged rock formations and to where the soft, billowing clouds offer gentle sweetness. Look around, feel around, and plant gardens and fields and ranges of whatever you most desire. Perhaps tulips represent brand new, and roses represent beauty, and daisies represent ... ??? And don't forget the trees. :) Did you ever notice that flowers and trees have the uncanny ability to grow anywhere??? Even from the smallest crack in the hardest stone...

Love your love,
Mary

Live life in the fast lane today. Get really zoomy! Take the corners with just the right amount of speed to feel the thrill of the exhilaration and yet keep you from flipping and rolling. Push it to the limit. No idling at the stop signs. Look both ways, make sure you won't run anything important over, and gun it! Woo-hoo! Oh, and leave the top down so you can feel the wind whipping through your soul. Let your open heart and spirit guide the way.

Skitching on your bumper,
Mary

L ove. Live. Laugh. Leap. Lounge. Linger. Launch. Land. Lead. Leak. Lollygag. Lend. Learn. And Listen.

Phew ... now that's a full day!

Loyally,
Mary

I t is a good day to shatter some old, limiting myths. Let us get you started: "Money doesn't grow on trees." This is untrue. Just ask an avocado farmer or the accountants for an orange juice company.

Today, weed your message garden. Remove the rubbish and plant imagination and possibility and willingness in their place.

Expanding the landscape,
Mary

What thoughts will you let gobble you up today? Oh, or will you realize that you can be the gobbler? Filling your own plate with the thoughts you choose to nourish yourself with. Talk about natural selection. Survival of the fittest: eat or be eaten. You eating the thoughts or letting the thoughts eat you.

The hunter or the hunted ... you chose.

Enjoying the feast,
Mary

Bring about change today. Any thought, reaction, or belief you have that doesn't feel good, change it. Oh, we know the temptation to justify it is packed with luring and feigned comfort and yet, we still urge you to change it instead of justifying it.

Begin the practice by changing the thought, reaction, or belief into love—love without agenda. If you are feeling bad, self-righteous, justified, angry, empty, jealous, resentful, defensive, etc. in union with any thought, reaction or belief moving through you today—change that thought, reaction, or belief to love. Remember, we are talking about pure love without agenda.

Morning Messages from Mary

In the end, love is all you are ever looking for to begin with so instead of attempting to force somebody or something outside of you to change to allow you to feel love—just begin by giving it to yourself and then without exception to the person or thing outside of you.

It's all about the shortcuts. You will find them inside every time. The direct route is always within. Choose to take the direct route to pure love today. In this case, taking the scenic view is long and unfulfilling and not very pretty to look at.

Offering,
Mary

P.S. No excuses.

Wiggle a little today. You know, let your body jiggle a bit from the shoulders down. Release those neck muscles and let your head bob a bit, too. Do it when you're walking, when you're talking, when you're sitting, when you're standing, when you're dressing, when you're confessing ... All day long as often as you think of it ... wiggle just a little. It loosens up the tight spots.

Ah, the "price" of freedom,
Mary

P.S. Oh, and not only when you're alone.

Today, live, choose, and actively engage your life in a way that allows you to feel your sense of satisfaction.

You know, that way-down-deep, expansive, delicious feeling of "Oh, yes—that's it—that feels good."

Your life is so tasty,
Mary

It is a most extraordinary thing, this movement of your life, isn't it? Whatever your current movement is. Wherever you take yourself with it. It is extraordinary. Do you get that?

We do. Join us, won't you?

Super-duper Love,
Mary

M eet you.

Dream you.

Be you.

Let this invitation be your offer to yourself today. Discover something inspiring about you in the practice of it.

Beaming,
Mary

B e with you today. Through all of the streams of thought, movements of choice, and expansions of belief, be with you today. Sink in, explore, and saturate. Know the wonder of you. Absorb what is true about you in your keenest observance of self and love every inch of your being with gusto and complete presence.

At least five times today, in the midst of your created moments, close your eyes for a moment, go inside and give yourself a hug.

Enjoying the embrace of you,
Mary

B eyond measure. Choose an aspect and offer it beyond measure today. Just close your eyes slowly, take in a deep breath, choose which aspect you would like to access and share ... love, hope, peace, joy, wonder, adoring, allowing ... and on the exhale, release its vibration, its essence, to emanate through you, caressing the entirety of self and then offering itself outward to either somebody or something in particular or for general access in the world.

The fun thing is, you don't even have to get dressed or go anywhere or physically encounter anyone to do it. And, it only takes an instant, so finding time won't be a difficulty. Or you can do it in the middle of a conversation that feels difficult or one that feels wonderful. You choose what you offer from the inside, no matter what is occurring on the outside. You really do.

Believing in you beyond measure,
Mary

Which way will you walk today?

Toward? Toward what?

Away? Away from what?

Make sure you are wearing comfy shoes,
Mary

What is a truth in the middle you? You know, a truth way past the surface, way past any spinning of it. What do you know that you know about you? Look inside today and find several of them. Let yourself see and know and be who you are in the space uninfluenced by outside circumstance.

Let us get you started:

> *I am Love*
>
> *I am Infinite*
>
> *I am ...*

You are the best book you will ever read, the grandest dance you will ever dance, the most exquisite tastiness you will ever enjoy ...

Dive in!
Mary

Be bright today. Let your light and your brilliance shine. Let the light of you hit and illuminate every corner of your internal and external world. And, let the brilliance of your mind soak it in for current and future reference. We suggest you turn the dimmer switch all the way up to your full light-emanating potential in this moment. Of course, that means you will have to keep turning it up, because with the embodiment of this practice, your potential keeps growing. Blinded by the Light ...

Good thing we have excellent sun glasses,
Mary

E ngage today. Whatever it is you choose to do, engage fully in it. Feel your day in all the fibers of your being, in all your particles, in all your cells, with all your might. Be present. BE. Magic is more noticeable and tangible when you are truly there to witness and experience it.

Lovingly shoving, nudging, pushing, pulling you—whatever it takes,
Mary

Open your mind, open your thoughts, open your heart, open your soul, your gifts, your love, your spirit, your joy, your trust, your fear (so you know what you're dealing with), open your whimsy, your belief, your truth, your humor, your listening, your understanding, your dream, your offering, your presence, your forgiveness, your vision, your caring, your magic, your acceptance, your celebration, your honoring, open yourself, open your today. OPEN.

Exhausting the excuses,
Mary

There is an elegance to life. Allow yourself to feel
the flow of it today.

Billowing,
Mary

Let your peace sweep and flow through you today. Let it scoop you up and lift you into your remembering that you are always well. Let it calm the ranting of your fears with its gentle and powerful embrace.

Allow your peace to assist you with allowing your answers to rise and find you with grace and ease.

That's it ... Let it in.

More than you know,
Mary

Morning Messages from Mary

Today, select something challenging from your past (a choice, a decision, an action, a regret ...) that with some consistency you bring into your present. Look at it clearly, give it a highly celebratory going-away party and leave it there ... in your past ... to hold its rightful space as a catalyst, not as a piece of baggage that you carry around with you.

When you have completed this task, repeat the process with something from the past from somebody else's story that with some consistency, you "hang over their head" (verbally or energetically) in the present.

Freeing your wings,
Mary

Choose an intention for your blinks today. Yep, that's what we said. Pick a thought, a desire, a belief, a wish that you would like to send out into your internal and external worlds every time you blink today. Like this: "I set an intention today that my ability to love purely will triple every time I blink." Or "I set an intention today that my 'yes' to my desires will open to release anything that holds me back with every blink."

Get it?

One a day keeps the doubt away,
Mary

P.S. Oh, and remember to agree with the intention to set it into motion.

t's because of you. The expanding love, the zooming possibility, the raging joy ... You did that. You are doing it right now ... adding to the particles that create your world. Share your wonder today. It doesn't take much. It really doesn't. Just you agreeing to let it rise within you and radiating.

Glow looks good on you,
Mary

Our dream is you. What is your dream?

Eyelids twitching in REM state,
Mary

L ife is _____ __

You fill in the blank and the punctuation mark. It's your life, after all. You decide. And then, live yourself through your choice with every breath today. Isn't it delicious? There are so many choices ... what will you choose???

On the edges of our seats as always,
Mary

Your love and your joy are showing. Do you feel them? Do you see them in every reflection? Do you give them permission? We mean, really, really give them permission ... unrestricted ... to be your guiding force in everything you do, say, encounter, think, believe, remember, begin... Yowza! Even the brilliance of the sun can't beat this one.

Squinting with pleasure as we adore you,
Mary

Today, live, choose, and actively engage your life in a way that allows you to feel your sense of satisfaction. You know, that way-down-deep, expansive, delicious feeling of "Oh, yes—that's it—that feels good."

Your life is so tasty,
Mary

It is a most extraordinary thing, this movement of your life, isn't it? Whatever your current movement is. Wherever you take yourself with it. It is extraordinary. Do you get that? We do. Join us, won't you?

Superduper Love,
Mary

Meet you. Dream you. Be you. Let this invitation be your offer to yourself today. Discover something inspiring about you in the practice of it.

Beaming,
Mary

Be with you today. Through all of the streams of thought, movements of choice and expansions of belief, be with you today. Sink in, explore and saturate. Know the wonder of you. Absorb what is true about you in your keenest observance of self and love every inch of your being with gusto and complete presence. At least five times today, in the midst of your created moments, close your eyes for a moment, go inside and give yourself a hug.

Enjoying the embrace of you,
Mary

Beyond measure. Choose an aspect and offer it beyond measure today. Just close your eyes slowly, take in a deep breath, choose which aspect you would like to access and share ... love, hope, peace, joy, wonder, adoring, allowing ... and on the exhale, release its vibration, its essence to emanate through you, caressing the entirety of self and then offering itself outward to either somebody or some thing in particular or for general access in the world.

The fun thing is, you don't even have to get dressed or go anywhere or physically encounter anyone to do it. And, it only takes an instant, so finding time won't be a difficulty. Or you can do it in the middle of a conversation that feels difficult or one that feels wonderful. You choose what you offer from the inside, no matter what is occurring on the outside. You really do.

Believing in you beyond measure,
Mary

What will you talk about today? Yourself, others, situations, events, the present, the future, the past ... ? Will your focus be on possibility, negativity, opportunity, success, defeat, joy, struggle, becoming ... ?

Remember that in every moment, you are choosing.

Be your dream.

Eyelids fluttering,
Mary

What is a truth in the middle you? You know, a truth way past the surface, way past any spinning of it. What do you know that you know about you?

Look inside today and find several of those truths. Let yourself see and know and be who you are in the space uninfluenced by outside circumstance. Let us get you started ... I am Love. I am Infinite. I am ...

You are the best book you will ever read, the grandest dance you will ever dance, the most exquisite tastiness you will ever enjoy...

Dive in!
Mary

Today, tell others why they matter to you. Let them know how they touch and ignite your life and in what way. Breathe them into your heart and let them live fully activated within you for the day. Notice and embrace the difference they make in your life. What spaces they occupy within your vibration, what gateways to you they have offered opening to. Love them with fierce purity. Love yourself with divine rapture.

Lather (dive in), Rinse (flow), Repeat (do it again ... and again ... and ... again,
Mary

Hop, skip, play, run, jump, prance, dance, zoom, varoom, be, glee, imagine, twirl, spin, bounce, tra la la, sing, dance, romance, believe, enjoy, hug, tug, laugh, love ... bigger, bigger, bigger ...

We know. Tall order. Good thing you are a GIANT.

Invincibly,
Mary

Let your heart be brand new today. Even if it is just a small fraction of it. Let it be refreshed, renewed, reopened. Let yourself gleam through its sparkle, shine through its hope, and radiate through its tenacious ability to love. See, think, feel and know through this space of you today.

Dreaming life with you,
Mary

What gets you going? What stirs and spins and burst within you? What of you will not resign itself to slumber or complacency or even entrapment? This is your force, your juice, your will. Let it LIVE! Let it THRIVE! Let it ENCAPSULATE YOU in its thrust and fly you to the moon and the stars and the divine dream of you.

Ohhhhhhhhhhhhhhhhhhhhhhhhhhh, SO delicious!
Mary

Offer ... Dream ... Become ... Decide ...
Endeavor ...

With all your might, with all your might. What is your "might," you ask? It is your vibration fueled by your will. Powerful fuel!

Firing up the engines,
Mary

My, oh my. My oh my ... The legions of spirit are coming together in a great gathering today, cranking up the volume on vibration and manifestation. Join us by cranking up your vibration and becoming very available for what matches it, won't you?

Titillated with anticipation,
Mary

P.S. Oh, you might want to pay attention to what it is you're vibrating to, just to make sure it is something you choose to match ...

Pay attention to what you can't hear, taste, touch, smell, see today.

Focus on your sixth sense ... vibration. Internally and externally. Doing this will allow you to hear, taste, touch, smell and see like never before!

From the knowing of no separation,
Mary

rder Up!

What did you order? Oh, we hope you picked your favorite thing! We hope you didn't skip over it for the sake of lack or worry and instead picked exactly what you wanted—really wanted. We hope you didn't settle for less than what struck you as the most delicious thing on the menu. Perhaps you even asked for it to be served tailored specifically to your taste ... Like "the dressing on the side please" or "please, oh please, add some extra whipped cream on that" ... Oh, and did you order a large enough portion to warrant extra spoons for sharing???

Mouths watering, bellies rumbling, glands salivating,
taste buds popping,
Mary

P.S. You do know the menu we are referring to is life, don't you? Always order what you truly desire!

Reach above, reach above. Above the complaint, the judgment, the frustration, the worry. Reach above the lure to create strong, powerful walls that keep you in much more profoundly than they will ever keep anything or anybody else out.

Reach out, reach out. Out into the absolute of all possibility, all choice, all wonder. Reach out into the invitation of discovery, hope and open flowing expansion.

Reach into, reach into. Into your heart, your love, your embrace, your juicy vibration. Reach into your allowing, your permission, your limitless radiance that will offer you more with each choice you make to feed it instead of deplete it.

Living in the spaces of you that are reaching and realized, Mary

Sparkles, sparks, glints, twinkling, lilts, tilts and whimsy—all characteristics of fairies, of wonder, of innocence. What measure of these things are you willing to let rise in you today? Before you answer consider the fact that you will have to decrease your attention to heavy, weighty, doom, gloom, worry, disallowing, control ... All it takes to change your world is the slightest pivot in what you pay attention to inside and outside.

Choosing, choosing. You are doing it all of the time.

Off to play on our boogie boards,
Mary

It's a good day to blow dandelion seeds. Inhale deeply, gather force from way down deep, and blow as hard as you can to send them flying in the breeze. Attach a wish to each seed as the seeds float in the air, fully knowing they will find their perfect places to land and come true, and in doing so, become the seedling to grow new wishes come true opportunities.

Floating on whimsy,
Mary

Hello! It is a great day! A stupendous day!

A love-soaking, rocket-flying, joy-inducing day!

Open. Let your heart know who you are and embrace all that matches you today. Just twirl right past the rest.

Spinning,
Mary

Today is a day to embody your dream of you. Be that which you desire yourself to be. Only that. Avoid temptation to act in any other way. It may require some deep breaths to bring you back to center before responding from time to time.

We will be right there with you, pulling for you all the way, believing in you beyond measure.

Pulsing in union with your vibration,
Mary

It is of great importance, that you tell yourself the truth. Every time. EVERY TIME. To whatever degree possible in each moment. Not so much your perception of the truth about others—though we know it is tempting, well practiced and serves as a great distraction, this is not your area of expertise. The truth about yourself—make that your area of expertise.

Practice this today in your thoughts, responses, reactions, choosing, belief, visioning ... "The truth about me in this moment is ..."

Ahhh, what a wonderful journey to self-fullness. We wish you an insightful experience. (Oh, and remember to pack your humor.)

Extraordinary love,
Mary

Fascinating, isn't it, the way you love? How you weave it through your heart, your soul, your mind, your body, your creativity, your wonder, your innocence, your truth, your splendor, your curiosity, your ... Infinite, really.

And that's just the way you love chocolate or a great bike ride or a moment of laughter ...

Today, captivate yourself with how you love each and every thing—starting with yourself.

Wrapping you with us in deep and abiding love,
Mary

Today, do something fresh. Something you have never done before or in a way you have never done it before. Use new energy, an adjusted vibration ... tilt a bit from the usual.

That is all it takes to change the world—inside and out.

Loving you infinitely,
Mary

Oh, and remember to tilt in the direction of what feeds your soul. Every time.

Be YES today.

We dare you.

Now that's vibrating!

Mary

Begin living the dream of you. Now. Today. Choose something. An aspect, a belief, a decision, a vision of self, a practice or perhaps even a shedding of a practice that is no longer in alignment with your desire of self of life and live it for a whole day. From the beginning of the day when your eyes first open to the end when you fall into peaceful slumber, live this thing you choose deliberately and consistently throughout your day. It will take some practice. It will take some remembering. It will take some choosing differently. It will take some dedication. It will take some thought ...

Experiencing ourselves in exchange with you in the purity of divine love,
Mary

E verything you need—everything—is right there inside of you. ALL the good stuff. Isn't that wonderful? Guess that's what they mean by "The best things in life are free." And to think ... the "store" you get them at, is you. Happy shopping! Use the giant cart.

Talk about being a "preferred customer"... "I'll have some of that, and some of that, and some of that ..."

Restocking the inventory with every selection,
Mary

(Don't we look cute in our stock clerk outfits),

Today be deliberate. Deliberately love, deliberately think, deliberately choose, deliberately respond, deliberately breath and move and believe and hope and dream and receive ...

Show up for every moment.

Life is so much richer when you are there for it.

Deliberately loving you,
Mary

B e porous today. Let everything move through you. If it feels good, let it linger a bit before continuing on its natural flow through. If it is contrary, skip the lingering part and just simply let it pass right through leaving nothing behind.

Rapture is porous. Pretty good company, we'd say.

Like the wind,
Mary

Open to amazement today. Really, really open to your aspect of amazement. Look through it, think through it, feel through it, breath through it. Let yourself be mesmerized by the wonder of it. You will know you are doing it when you feel the dancing in every particle of your existence.

Building the dance floor for you,
Mary

What is the truth in you? About anything. Ask yourself lots of questions about you today or at least one or two and answer with the truth.

Remember we are saying ask questions—not question yourself ... BIG difference.

Get to know you. You are fabulous!

Scooping you up in love,
Mary

Today, seek opportunities to love yourself. Look for you in everything you experience and reach out and in to you with love.

Fingertips,
Mary

Breathe calmness into your inner turmoil, wrestlings, and confusions today. Allow the smooth, steady flow of your breath to move through the conflicted spaces, opening you to recognitions of limitless options and releasing you from old stories that no longer serve you.

Love.

Peace.

Zoom.

Live.

Immediate and enduring,
Mary

Give birth to life today. New life. Your new life. Change a pattern, a belief, a decision, a practice. Meet yourself there, shake your hand in introduction and receive the goodness ... the richness of your own friendship ... your own embrace.

Believing in your dream of you,
Mary

Receive today. Yep, soak it all in. Let every inhale pull in the goodness of life.

YUM!
Mary

One thousand time one thousand times "YES!" You are doing it exactly right! All of it!

Today, release your questioning—completely. Replace this practice with asking questions, telling yourself the truth, and actively choosing.

Ah, yes ... we just felt the breath of expansion exhale across the Universe.

Ride the wave,
Mary

Every day, love more. In every situation.

Imagine a world where love is always the first response. Take a moment to breathe that in. Feel its vibration. Bask in it.

Now, start doing it. And never stop.

Always and forever,
Mary

Whatever it is that is dragging you down or holding you back or causing you to disbelieve—to stand, live, breathe in any measure separate from your complete realization of your vision, arrange a farewell party and send it packing.

It's time to fly without anchors.

Weightless levitating love,
Mary

Catch yourself controlling today. Yep, just observe it. Notice you do it (internally and externally). And then consider taking deep breaths to move you through your need to do it quite so often. With every inhale expand your sense of well-being and trust. With every exhale, release your rigidity and yielding.

Like a bowl full of cherries,
Mary

Caution: Some of you may hyperventilate from all the deep breathing. Carry a small brown bag with you. :)

C herish this day.

Cherish yourself.

Cherish your moments.

Cherish every expression, every breath, every experience, every living particle in it.

Truly cherish. It will change your life. You have everything you need to do it right there within you.

Loving you more every moment,
Mary

What is in your weaving? Who is in your weaving? Consider just one person or experience in your life. What led to them or it manifesting in your life? What choices, what thoughts, what actions, what releases, what allowing, what tools (this includes other people) ... went into your creation?

When you take an in-depth look at just one, you will realize how infinite and fun possibility and routes to manifestation really are. Let it inspire you to keep believing in the "impossible."

With sugar on top,
Mary

The next time you decide to believe in inequity, choose another perspective. That is ... if you want to tell yourself the truth.

In perfect harmony,
Mary

ount the number of stars that live within you. Feel their warm, sparkling delight. Then make a wish on each of them. At least one a day. Write each wish down and carry it with you.

Starlight, Star Bright
First star I see tonight
I wish I may, I wish I might
Have the wish I wish tonight.

Remember, these stars are right there inside of you, and they have corresponding stars that burn in the sky outside of you. Feel the power of your connectivity and match to the grandness of the Universe and realize the full nature of your ability to tap in and ignite your every wish to coming true. Created by you, supported by the Universe.

Remember ... the wish is the catalyst. Fuel it with your passionate commitment to its manifestation and your complete and practiced willingness to be that which you desire to experience.

Soaring love,
Mary

P.S. Stars are brilliantly burning all the time, not just when you can see them.

Tap into wisdom today. Sink into the warm, enveloping comfort of it and let it rise to meet your moments. Let it assist you with finding truth much more quickly, readily and willingly. Wisdom has no argument or contrariness with life. It moves consistently with recognition, understanding, and deepening insight. It knows full awareness without judgment or fear regarding all which is internal and external.

Try it on. Feel its glove-like fit.

Surfing the contours,
Mary

Sit with Love today. All of it. Yours. Ours. "Theirs." Allow it to know you well.

Saturating,
Mary

Feel and experience your arch point today. Allow yourself to know the freedom of your vibrational connection to everything. Each time you encounter another today, meet them from the center of your high heart—the space of activated loving—and observe what the moment evokes and emanates from you. Imagine an arch of your brilliant, piercing light moving from the center of your existence, arching slightly as it skims the bottom of your chin and flies forward to embrace all of the wonder of the other.

Or live on the surface. Your choice.

Gleaming,
Mary

In Closing ...

It is my hope that the soul-expanding words and penetrating inspirations Mary has offered throughout this book will find their way into your heart and daily practice of living, birthing a new energy and edgeless, ecstatic existence, as they have mine, Don's, and those of many others around the world.

It has been a staggeringly honoring experience to be gifted by the words and love of "The Marys" coming through me. I am humbled each time one of the recipients of their teachings has shared some measure of a life-opening shift or personal story of transformation he or she has experienced as a result of having encountered Mary. Each story graces my heart with the immense beauty of knowing that what each of us does offers to the whole of Creation through the expression of love. Love knows the way and the place to land for perfect unfolding.

I am so grateful, through the support of my family and

friends, to be able to offer my piece and practice of God, the Oneness, the All That Is, to the world in such a heart-filling way.

My heart to yours,
Jacque

The Mary Group

Don and Jacque Nelson are ecstatic to continue bringing Mary to the world. They offer this opportunity through a variety of formats:

μ   Partial and full-day seminars
μ   Week-long adventure journeys with Mary
μ   Newsletters
μ   Morning Messages from Mary via email
μ   Private sessions (limited schedule)

To learn more about Mary or to find out how you can find yourself in a personal audience with them, either in a group or privately, or to bring them to your area, please visit: www.themarygroup.com or call The Inner Vortex/ The Mary Group at (815) 623-1475.

Forthcoming books by Jacque Nelson and The Mary Group from Radiant Heart Press include:

μ   Living Without Edges: An Inspired Journey into Mary's Teachings from the Loft View

μ   Living in the Absence of Fear: Embracing a Life of Peace and Freedom

μ   Morning Message Journals